Colonial America

Building Toward Independence

Titles in *The American Saga* series

The Abolition of Slavery
Fighting for a Free America
0-7660-2605-1

America as a World Power
From the Spanish-American War to Today
0-7660-2606-X

Colonial America
Building Toward Independence
0-7660-2569-1

The History of U.S. Immigration
Coming to America
0-7660-2574-8

The Industrial Revolution
Manufacturing a Better America
0-7660-2571-3

The New Deal
Pulling America Out of the Great Depression
0-7660-2570-5

The Struggle for Equality
Women and Minorities in America
0-7660-2573-X

**The Transcontinental Railroad and
Westward Expansion**
Chasing the American Frontier
0-7660-2572-1

Colonial America

Building Toward Independence

Richard Worth

 Enslow Publishers, Inc.
40 Industrial Road
Box 398
Berkeley Heights, NJ 07922
USA

http://www.enslow.com

Library of Congress Cataloging-in-Publication Data

Worth, Richard.
    Colonial America: building toward independence / Richard Worth.
      p. cm. — (The American saga)
    Includes bibliographical references and index.
    ISBN 0-7660-2569-1
      1. United States—History—Colonial period, ca. 1600–1775—Juvenile literature. I. Title. II. Series.
    E188.W67 2006
    973.2—dc22

                                  2005016432

Printed in the United States of America

10 9 8 7 6 5 4 3 2 1

To Our Readers:
We have done our best to make sure all Internet Addresses in this book were active and appropriate when we went to press. However, the author and the publisher have no control over and assume no liability for the material available on those Internet sites or on other Web sites they may link to. Any comments or suggestions can be sent by e-mail to comments@enslow.com or to the address on the back cover.

Illustration Credits: Clipart.com, pp. 32, 33, 60; © Corel Corporation, p. 98; Engraved by Charles Pye after a painting by Sir Antonio More, reproduced from the *Dictionary of American Portraits*, published by Dover Publications, Inc., in 1967, pp. 15, 113 (top); Enslow Publishers, Inc., pp. 14, 95; Getty Images, pp. 22, 44, 74; J. S. Peterson @ USDA-NRCS PLANTS Database, p. 24; The Library of Congress, pp. 3, 10, 27, 37, 49, 56, 57, 71, 76, 90, 92, 102, 104, 110, 111, 113 (middle and bottom), 114 (middle), 115; ©Mary Evans Picture Library / The Image Works, pp. 19, 34, 84; The National Archives and Records Administration, pp. 6, 85, 97, 107; North Wind Picture Archives, p. 16; Photos.com, p. 17; Courtesy Princeton University Archives, reproduced from the *Dictionary of American Portraits*, published by Dover Publications, Inc., in 1967, p. 7; Smithsonian Institution, pp. 42, 53, 61, 78, 89, 94, 101, 109, 114 (top and bottom); The U.S. Mint, p. 11.

Cover Illustration: The Library of Congress (inset); "Patrick Henry before the Virginia House of Burgesses (1851) by Peter P. Rothermel. Red Hill, Patrick Henry National Memorial, Brookneal, Virginia.

Contents

The Declaration of Independence outlined the rights that the colonists believed they deserved and announced their separation from Great Britain.

A Declaration

The humid summer heat in 1776 filled the rooms of the Pennsylvania State House in Philadelphia as sixty-five delegates debated the future of their nation. The delegates at the Second Continental Congress had begun meeting in May 1775, more than a year earlier. The armies of Great Britain and the American colonies had already battled in Massachusetts. Yet, some of the men at the Congress still wanted to go slow. Led by Pennsylvania delegate John Dickinson, they hoped to mend relations with England and avoid a long war.

Some of the delegates represented successful merchants who had prospered as part of the British Empire. They appreciated the protection their ships received from the British navy. Others were afraid that the Americans could not stand up to the British army, the world's most powerful military force. This group, the majority, gave Dickinson their approval to send a petition to the British king, George III. It was

John Dickinson tried to avoid war with Britain. He made sure to get this point across when he represented Pennsylvania in the Second Continental Congress.

aimed at ending the differences between Great Britain and the American colonies.

Nevertheless, a small group of delegates believed the time had come to declare independence. They were led by Massachusetts delegate John Adams, a bald, heavy-set, plainspoken lawyer. Adams also had the support of Thomas Jefferson, a young, handsome plantation owner and political leader from Virginia. While the delegates had been meeting during the winter, an American expedition had invaded British territory in Canada. Many Americans believed that the Canadians would rise up against the British government. But the American army was defeated in a blizzard as it attacked the British stronghold at Quebec.

Many delegates believed that the attack had failed because Congress had not been fully committed to war. Meanwhile, King George III had rejected the delegates' petition, calling on his armies to crush the rebellious colonies. By spring 1776, word had also reached the Congress that Britain had hired Hessians to fight in America against the colonists. These hired soldiers, called mercenaries, were from a region of Germany and had a reputation for brutality.

By May 1776, an overwhelming majority of the delegates had finally given their support to independence. John Adams initiated a resolution stating that "the exercise of every kind of authority under the said Crown should be totally suppressed, and all sources of government exerted under the authority of the people."[1] In June, Richard Henry Lee, a delegate from

Virginia, introduced a resolution stating that the American colonies "are, and of right ought to be, free and independent States. . . ."[2] This resolution was discussed by the delegates, and a committee was appointed to write a Declaration of Independence. The committee included Thomas Jefferson, known for his writing skills, Adams, and Benjamin Franklin, a delegate from Pennsylvania.

After Jefferson had carefully composed a Declaration of Independence, the committee presented it to the other delegates on June 28, 1776. The declaration was based in part on the writings of John Locke, a seventeenth-century English philosopher. Locke had declared that the duty of every government was to protect the rights

"We hold these truths to be self-evident, that all men are created equal, that they are endowed by their Creator with certain unalienable Rights, that among these are Life, Liberty and the pursuit of Happiness."

—The words of the Declaration of Independence echoed many of John Locke's own ideas.

of its citizens. When these rights were severely undermined, Locke said, citizens had the right to overthrow their government. Since the seventeenth century, each of the colonies had defended what Locke called the right to "life, health, liberty, or possessions." In fact, Locke

Benjamin Franklin (left), John Adams (center), and Thomas Jefferson worked on the Declaration of Independence. Jefferson wrote most of the document, completing several drafts before he was satisfied with the text.

had written the constitution for the Carolina colonies, based on these identical beliefs.

Since that time, each of the colonies had elected its own independent legislature, which decided what taxes should be levied on every citizen. The colonists enjoyed free speech, the right to publish their opinions, and freedom from any army being quartered in their homes. However, all of these freedoms were jeopardized by actions of the British Parliament during the 1760s and 1770s.

Jefferson described this situation in his draft of the declaration. After debate, the delegates voted. Nine colonies now supported independence. This was a majority. But the delegates wanted the vote to be unanimous, as a show of greater strength to encourage all Americans to join the struggle for freedom. Perhaps, as Franklin put it, "we must indeed all hang together, or most assuredly we shall all hang separately."[3] As the delegates prepared for another vote, messages arrived that the British forces were advancing against New York. The delegates from South Carolina, one of the holdouts, now favored independence.

The little colony of Delaware had been undecided in the first vote. One delegate favored independence, another was opposed,

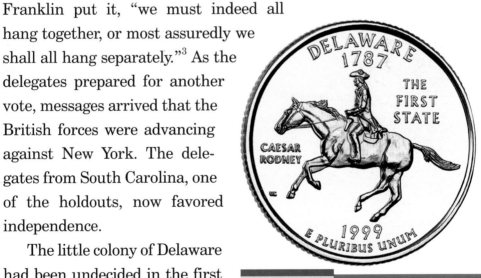

Caesar Rodney is honored on the back of Delaware's state quarter.

and the third, Caesar Rodney, was absent. Before the next vote, Rodney, a supporter of independence, rode eighty miles through a fierce thunderstorm from Delaware to Philadelphia. He arrived just in time to vote in favor of independence on July 2. Pennsylvania and New York, other holdouts, also gave their support to independence.

On July 4, 1776, Congress adopted the Declaration of Independence. Soon afterward it was announced publicly. This was a crucial moment that put Americans on a new and dangerous path into the future. As one contemporary put it, who wrote under the pen name Civis, this was a "leap into the dark."[4]

However, the foundations of independence had begun to be laid more than a century and a half earlier. From the earliest days of colonial America, the new settlers were striving to assert their freedoms and govern themselves.

Opening a New Land

During the last part of the 1500s, Great Britain established its first colony in North America. Over the next century, thousands of British settlers would build towns along the Atlantic coast. Although the colonists remained intensely loyal to Britain, they also planted the seeds that flowered into independence.

Colony at Roanoke

Britain was not the first European country to develop colonies in the New World. During the first half of the sixteenth century, Spain had conquered wealthy empires in Mexico and South America. The Spanish found vast treasures of gold and silver, which were shipped back to Spain. Along the way, some of the treasure ships were attacked by British sea captains. Led by Sir Francis Drake and Sir John Hawkins, British sailors pirated Spanish gold and silver, taking it back to Britain.

Eventually Hawkins, Drake, and others decided that Britain should establish its own colonies in America. They formed an investment group that was led by Sir Walter Raleigh. Known for his good looks,

Settlements by 1700

Huron Villages

Lake Huron

Caciaque

Lake Ontario

Iroquois Villages

Salem
Boston
Plymouth
Providence

Chippewa Villages

Ottawa Villages

Otinawaiawa

Albany

Lake Michigan

Lake Erie

Kickapoo Villages

Susquehannock Villages

Hudson R.

Susquehanna R.

Boston

Post Rd

New York

Miami Villages

Ohio R.

Philadelphia

Post

Chesapeake Bay

Atlantic Ocean

Mississippi R.

Illinois R.

Shawnee Villages

Fort Henry

James R.

Main

Ohio R.

Cherokee Villages

Chiaha

Xuala

Otavi

Pacaha

Mississippi R.

Tennessee R.

Road

N
W E
S

Chicaca (Chickasaw Villages)

Coca

Culitatchiqui

Main

Post

Charles Town

Choctaw Villages

Port Royal

Cabusto

Chattahoochee R.

Aminoya

Mavila

Apalachee

Main

Saint Augustine

Ocale

Ocita

Gulf of Mexico

Key

★ Fort
• Town
🏚 American Indian Village
— Road
▨ Extent of settled area, 1700

Settlement of the present-day United States began as early as the 1500s; however, by 1700, only a small portion of the land had been settled.

his wit, and his pleasing manners, Raleigh was a close friend of Britain's queen, Elizabeth I. The investors decided to name their colony Virginia, after the queen. Elizabeth was known as the Virgin Queen because she never married.

Between 1585 and 1587, Raleigh tried to establish settlements at Roanoke, in present-day North Carolina. Unfortunately, these settlements suffered from food shortages and conflicts with American Indians. The only trace of the final settlement was a single word written on a tree. That word was CROATOAN.

Sir Walter Raleigh was greatly interested in establishing a colony at Roanoke. The British hoped to use the colony as a naval base for fighting their enemy—Spain.

Perhaps the settlers sought food and shelter from the nearby Croatoan tribe. Or perhaps they had been killed by the Croatoans. Ever since that time, historians have been puzzled about the fate of the colonists. Indeed, Roanoke became known as the Lost Colony.

American Indians of the Atlantic Region

As the British established their first colonies, they continued to have encounters with the American Indians. Many small, independent tribes lived along the Atlantic coast. All of them spoke Algonquian

Despite many searches, the ultimate fate of the Roanoke colonists has never been discovered. Their last days remain one of the greatest mysteries of American history.

languages. They were among the one million to two million American Indians who lived east of the Mississippi River during the sixteenth century. Over the next century, many Indians died. European settlers brought diseases such as the flu, measles, and smallpox. The American Indians had never been exposed to these diseases, so their immune systems—which fight off illnesses—did not protect them.[1] One Roanoke colonist, Thomas Hariot, wrote about how the Indians thought the colonists were having their god kill them. "They were persuaded that it was the work of our God through our means, and that we by him might kill and slay whom we would without weapons and not come near them."[2]

The Algonquian lived in small villages of about thirty homes each. Several centuries earlier, they had developed a very successful method of farming. In fields surrounding their villages, they planted corn, beans, and squash. The three crops grew together in small mounds. As the corn stalk grew, the bean plants wrapped themselves around the stalks. Beans provided nitrogen to enrich and fertilize the soil. The broad leaves of the squash plants spread themselves over the

The American Indians' main crop was corn. Sometimes they dried it and ground it into cornmeal.

soil to keep out weeds from damaging the beans and corn. These three plants were known as the Three Sisters. However, the most important crop was corn. In fact, the Indians held a huge celebration each fall when the corn was harvested.

One of the most highly prized values among clan or village members was sharing. American Indians did not believe in individual ownership of the land or the fields. The Indians worked them together and shared in the harvest. When the land was no longer fertile, the Indians moved on and established another village. Even their chiefs were not expected to pile up possessions. As one observer put it, "The chiefs are generally the poorest among them, for instead of their receiving anything . . . these Indian chiefs are made to give to the populace."[3]

In addition to the Algonquian tribes, other American Indian groups also lived east of the Mississippi River. In the southern part of the continent lived the Creek, Choctaw, and Chickasaw, who spoke a similar language. They established villages and farms much like the Algonquians.

Northward, stretching across present-day New York, were the Iroquois tribes. They included five Indian nations—Mohawk, Oneida, Onondaga, Cayuga, and Seneca. Later they were joined by the Tuscaroras. About 1600, the Iroquois population numbered around 20,000 people.[4] Like the other Indians, the Iroquois had established farms based on the Three Sisters. They built rectangular homes, known as longhouses, where men lived with their wives' families. Indeed, women had so much power among the Iroquois that they selected the tribal chiefs.

The chiefs of the Iroquois nations worked together in a form of government unlike those of other American Indians. It was called the Iroquois Confederacy. The confederacy was probably founded during the fifteenth century by two Indians. They were Deganawida, known as the Peacemaker, and Hiawatha,

Hiawatha helped start the Iroquois Confederacy, which was a form of democracy, or rule by the people.

a chief of the Mohawks. Together these two men ended the conflicts between the five nations by convincing the chiefs to work together. As the Deganawida put it, their purpose was to form a government in which "thinking will replace violence."[5]

At Onondaga, the capital of the Confederacy, fifty chiefs met together. Frequently, their warriors fought together against an enemy that threatened one of the Iroquois groups. The Confederacy gave the Iroquois an important advantage over other American Indians because they had a single government and the combined military power of five nations.[6]

Under the rules of the Confederacy, the Iroquois nations were expected to live in peace with each other. They acted as a single unit to deal with other nations. To make decisions, the Seneca and the Mohawk met together as one "house." The Oneida, Cayuga, and Tuscarora met as another "house." If both Iroquois houses were not in agreement, then the Onondaga broke the tie.

The Iroquois recognized the importance of acting together. This gave them enormous power in defending themselves against enemies. During the seventeenth century, these enemies would become far more powerful. The Iroquois, as well as other American Indian tribes, would be challenged by British colonists.

The New English Settlements

In 1606, a group of well-to-do London merchants formed the Virginia Company. They wanted to establish a new colony in North America. In December 1606, three ships left England (part of Great Britain) with about one hundred colonists, bound for the New World. In April 1607, they sailed into the Chesapeake Bay. The colonists began exploring one of the rivers that emptied into the bay. The colonists named this river the James, after King James I of England. On the river, they established a new colony, called Jamestown, in what is today the state of Virginia. Unfortunately, Jamestown was in a swampy area. Mosquitoes carried malaria that began to kill the colonists. About one-third died in less than a year. As one observer put it, "Instead of a plantacion [*sic*], Virginia will shortly get the name of a slaughterhouse."[1]

Disease was not the only problem that faced the colonists. Instead of planting crops, most of the settlers were far more eager to search for gold. Captain John Smith, an early leader of the colony, remarked,

Upon landing at Jamestown, settlers had to build houses and a fort to protect themselves from possible American Indian attack. Many Indians were angry with the colonists for taking their land.

"There was no talke, no hope, nor worke, but dig gold, wash gold, [and] refine gold."[2] Instead of gold, the colonists found only mica—a shiny, silver rock that had no value. Smith finally persuaded the colonists to get to work and plant crops.

Meanwhile, the settlers tried to persuade a local Algonquian Indian group to give them food. The group was ruled by Chief Powhatan. At first, Powhatan tried to help the settlers. He hoped to trade with them and, in turn, receive their assistance to deal with enemy tribes. However, Powhatan's people grew little surplus food and needed most of these crops to feed themselves.

When the settlers kept demanding more and more food, the American Indians killed some of the colonists. They wanted to drive the colonists off Indian hunting grounds. In retaliation, the settlers attacked Indian villages in 1610, burning crops and killing innocent women and children. Three years later, the settlers captured Pocahontas, daughter of Powhatan. After she was taken to Jamestown, Pocahontas met John Rolfe, one of the colonists. Rolfe wanted to marry Pocahontas, and Chief Powhatan agreed because he thought it would improve relations between the Indians and the colonists. The marriage in 1614 helped create peace between the Jamestown settlers and the American Indians. Rolfe and his wife later went to England. Pocahontas died there in 1617 at age twenty-one.

Tobacco

Meanwhile, back in Virginia, Rolfe had begun growing tobacco, a crop that proved to be as valuable as gold for the colonists. Tobacco had been grown in North America by the American Indian tribes. Rolfe began planting tobacco in 1616. Colonists in Virginia grew two hundred thousand pounds of tobacco in the early 1620s. By 1638, Virginia was producing 3 million pounds.[3] Tobacco was planted in the spring. The plants needed constant care to prevent caterpillars and other pests from attacking them. In the fall, the plants were harvested. The leaves were dried, and then placed into barrels for the long trip to England.

Tobacco plantations required many workers to tend

Tobacco is still grown in
Virginia today.

the fields. To attract more settlers, the Virginia
Company established a new form of government in the
colony. It included a governor, a council of advisors, and
a legislature, called the House of Burgesses. The House
of Burgesses held its first meeting in 1619. This was the
first time a colonial legislature, or group of lawmakers,
met in North America. No similar legislatures were created in the Spanish or French colonies in the New
World. All males were permitted to vote. In Britain, by
contrast, only well-to-do property owners could vote for

members of parliament. As historian Richard Middleton wrote, "[Virginia] set the pattern for government which within two centuries led to genuine democracy."[4]

However, many people were still reluctant to leave Britain and head into an unknown wilderness. The trip across the Atlantic often took twelve weeks. The voyagers crossed stormy seas that made many passengers seasick. In addition, they were forced to eat a steady diet of salted meat and bread. Frequently the food became infested with worms during the voyage. Many settlers also could not afford the cost of a voyage. In England, they held low-paying jobs working as laborers on farms owned by well-to-do aristocrats or they were unemployed.

As a result, those who wanted to go to America were often forced to travel as indentured servants. Ship captains paid their passage. Then the captains sold the servants to planters in Virginia. The white servants were then forced to work on the plantation for a period of four to seven years. They put in long days in the tobacco fields, battling hot weather and hordes of insects. Indentured servants lived in small cabins. These cabins usually had no windows and only a small fireplace. The fires enabled the colonists to cook their meals and keep themselves warm in the winter.

When the period of indenture was over, the former servants were given land—as much as three hundred acres. They could establish their own tobacco plantations. On these plantations, farmers earned far more than the average worker in England. Instead of working for someone else, like so many of the peasants in England, they could also become their own masters. As historian Alan Taylor wrote, "The ownership of productive land endowed men with the coveted condition of 'independence,' free at last from the dictates of a master. Their new independence enabled many to acquire their own dependents: wives, children, and servants."[5] This helped lay the foundation for political independence from Great Britain in the eighteenth century.

New England Colonies

While colonies were being established in the South, settlers were also sailing to the colder, northern climate of New England. Many of these settlers were motivated by religious beliefs. In England, Protestant religious groups known as Puritans wanted to change the Church of England, which was also Protestant. Among other things, they believed that the worship service was far too much like that of the Catholic Church. (During the sixteenth century, Protestants had broken away from the Catholic Church and set up their own religions.) In addition Puritans believed that the Church of England had too many high-ranking members of the clergy. These bishops and archbishops were much like the leaders of the Catholic Church. Some of the Puritans hoped to remain in the Church of England and reform it. Others, known as Separatists, had become convinced that they must leave the Church of England. They wanted to start their own religion.

Pilgrims and Puritans

Among the Separatists was a group of colonists. They, along with other adventurous people from Britain, sailed to New England in 1620 on the *Mayflower*. These 102 colonists have come to be known as the Pilgrims. Before coming ashore, the Pilgrims drew up and signed the Mayflower Compact. This was the first written form of government in the English colonies. The Pilgrims had heard about the problems of Jamestown. Settlers did not always follow the directions of leaders like Captain John Smith. The pilgrims wanted to avoid these problems with a written framework of government that would

Before they even stepped on land, the Pilgrims made sure that they had some form of government and set of laws in the Mayflower Compact.

bind all the colonists. Every male colonist was required to sign the compact and follow its rules.

The Pilgrims established a colony at Plymouth, along the coast of present-day Massachusetts. With the help of a local Algonquian group known as the Wampanoag, the Pilgrims learned how to plant the Three Sisters. The Wampanoag leader, Massasoit, hoped to trade with the Pilgrims. He also wanted to enlist their help to fight some of his enemies. In the autumn of 1621, the Pilgrims harvested their first crops. Then, they celebrated the first Thanksgiving with the Wampanoag.

There were only a small number of English Separatists. Therefore, the colony at Plymouth had reached only three hundred people by 1630.[6] That same year, a well-to-do group of Puritans and their families left England. They established a new settlement at Boston, Massachusetts. Led by John Winthrop, an English landowner, the Puritans set up the Company of Massachusetts Bay. Under the company charter issued by King Charles I, the government of Massachusetts Bay included a governor, an advisory council, and a legislature known as the general court. The headquarters of the company was located, not in England, like that of other colony companies, but in Massachusetts. This provided the colonial leaders with greater freedom and independence to run their own government.

Their government, the Puritans hoped, would be guided by the principles of God. Thus, the Puritans hoped to create a purer society than any that existed in

Europe. Indeed, the Puritans saw their colony as a "city on a hill." To them, it was a beacon of purity, in contrast to the sinfulness that they felt existed in England. They were inspired by their religion to achieve a practical goal—building a new society in the wilderness of New England. At the same time, they hoped to be rewarded not only on earth but also in heaven.

Puritans believed in hard work and devotion to God. "We teach that only Doers shall be saved," they said.[7] Each family who came to the Massachusetts Bay colony received their own land to farm. This enabled them to experience a sense of independence. Most remained around Boston. Others drifted northward into the present-day states of New Hampshire and Maine. As historian Alan Taylor wrote:

> Diligent and realistic, most New England families
> sought an "independent competency."
> "Independence" meant owning enough
> property—a farm or a shop—to employ a family
> without having to work for someone else as a
> hired hand or servant. A "competency" meant a
> sufficiency, but not an abundance, of worldly
> goods: enough to eat, adequate if simple clothing,
> a roof over their heads. . . .[8]

In addition to owning shops and farms, some New Englanders became fishermen off the coast. Others worked as shipbuilders. Many farmers and tradesmen made extra money that they used to purchase goods, such as sugar and tobacco. These products were transported to the colony from abroad.

New England's leaders encouraged an independent competency. But they did not permit any independence in religious beliefs. Colonists were expected to abide by Puritan doctrines. Men had to be members of the Puritan church, known as the Congregational Church, in order to vote for members of the legislature. The laws passed by the legislature required Puritans to attend two long sermons at church every Sunday. They were also expected to attend another church service on Thursday. Those who disagreed with the Puritan religion were banished from the colony.

"We teach that only doers shall be saved."

—Puritan belief that only those who
work hard will go to heaven.

Some of these colonists, such as Roger Williams, founded new colonies based on religious freedom and the separation of church and state. This meant that the government should not require any citizens to worship in only one way and should not support any church with their taxes. The ideals of religious freedom and the separation of church and state became part of the American Constitution, written in 1787.

Puritans and American Indians

At first, the Puritans seemed content to live side by side with the local American Indians. Gradually, more and more settlers arrived, who established more farms. They cut down trees and reduced forests that were home to deer and other animals. The Indians depended on these animals for food. The colonists also raised pigs that ran loose and destroyed the Indians' cornfields. When some Indians struck back and killed these animals, they were hauled into court by the Puritans.

The Indians were forced to pay their fines in wampum. This was a form of Indian money, made from the shells of fish along the Atlantic coast. The Indians also paid in furs, which were trapped away from the coast. In Europe, there was a great demand for beaver fur to make hats. However, more and more coins from Europe came into circulation in North America. As a result, the value of wampum decreased. Instead of paying their fines in wampum or fur, the Indians gave their lands to the Puritans.

As the Narragansett chief Miantonomo put it:

> Our fathers had plenty of deer and skins, our
> plains were full of deer, as also our woods, and of
> turkeys, and our coves full of fish and fowl. But
> these English have gotten our land, they with
> scythes cut down the grass, and with axes fell
> the trees; their cows and horses eat the grass,
> and their hogs spoil our clam banks, and we shall
> all be starved.[9]

In 1637, war broke out in Connecticut between the colonists and the Pequot, a local American Indian group. The Pequot were destroyed, and their land confiscated by the settlers.

Roger Williams (c1603–1683) and Anne Hutchinson (1591–1643)

Two people who broke away from the Puritans were Anne Hutchinson and Roger Williams. They both were unique people who helped start the colony of Rhode Island.

Born about 1603, Williams graduated from Cambridge University in England in 1627. Trained as a clergyman, he sailed for New England late in 1630. However, he was uncomfortable with the Puritan government there. He criticized the Puritan leaders for taking land from the American Indians. Williams also disagreed with their view that everyone in the colony should abide by the same religious beliefs. Instead Williams believed in "soul-liberty." This meant that every person could find God in his or her own way.

In 1635, Williams was banished from Massachusetts Bay. He fled southward, where he was given land by the local Indians. Williams founded the colony of Providence, which became part of present-day Rhode Island. Providence colony was built on the principle of religious toleration and the separation of church and state.

Anne Marbury was born in England in 1591. At age 21, she married Will Hutchinson. In 1634, she and her husband, together with their fifteen children, sailed to New England. They hoped to find religious freedom in Massachusetts. Anne Hutchinson believed that she could find God simply through her faith, without conforming to all the regulations of Puritanism.

She also believed that women were not inferior to men. However, most Puritan males disagreed with her. She was criticized by the Puritan leaders for expressing her views. They stated that these opinions were "not tolerable nor comely in the sight of God, nor fitting for your sex."[10] When she refused to change her views, Anne Hutchinson was arrested. Then she was banished from the colony in 1637, and fled to the Providence colony founded by Roger Williams.

Another conflict broke out in the 1670s. It was a war against the Wampanoag, and their chief, Metacomet. He was known by the name King Philip among the colonists. The conflict was called King Philip's War. Born about 1640, Metacomet was a son or grandson of Massasoit. At first, Metacomet cooperated with the English settlers. He wanted their help to defeat some of the enemies of his tribe. Metacomet also benefited from trade with the English. His people acquired copper kettles and muskets by trading wampum with the colonists. Gradually, the wampum became worth less and less. The Wampanoag had to sell land for the English trade goods. Often, they were forced to sell at very low prices.

In 1675, the Wampanoag attacked New England towns. They hoped to drive the English off their former hunting grounds. They destroyed twelve towns, wiping out men, women, and children. Gradually, the Puritans fought back with the help of American Indians who were enemies

Growing up as a Wampanoag, Metacomet saw the colonists gradually take more and more land from his people.

European Trade Changes the Lives of American Indians

European settlers introduced a variety of trade goods that they exchanged for furs with the American Indians. These new items changed the lifestyle of Indians. In the past, Indians had carried hot coals in a clay container from one place to another so they could start new fires for cooking. The colonial traders introduced flint and steel "strike-a-lights." By rubbing the flint and steel together, the Indians could start a fire anywhere.

Copper kettles made cooking easier. In the past, Indians had used clay pots that could break easily. Hot rocks were placed in the pots to heat soup or other food. Kettles could be kept simmering over a fire all day without breaking, as the clay pots did.

Iron awls replaced those made of sharp stone. With these awls, Indians could carve many more beads to produce far more wampum. According to one estimate, three million wampum beads had been made in the lands of the Iroquois by 1650.[11] This dramatically reduced the value of wampum.

Metal points on arrows replaced stone. New metal points made arrows sharper and more dangerous. Finally, the traders introduced firearms—muskets—that changed Indian warfare. American Indians became very dependent on the new trading items. Indeed, they traded away their lands to be able to have a continuous supply of these items in their villages.

of the Wampanoag. The American Indians taught the colonists how to fight Indian style. This meant slipping through the woods, ambushing the enemy, and burning their crops. In 1676, Metacomet was killed. His people were gradually defeated and enslaved by the colonists. More settlers came to New England, where the population grew from about 52,000 at the time of war to 92,000 in 1700.[12]

Middle Colonies

Growth was also occurring in the Middle Colonies—
Delaware, New York, New Jersey, and Pennsylvania.
New York, originally called New Netherland, was settled by the Dutch during the 1620s and 1630s. Dutch
settlers not only established farms, but also carried on
a thriving fur trade with the Iroquois Indians. Dutch
and Swedish settlers also established towns in present-
day Delaware. In 1664, New Netherland, Delaware,
and New Jersey were conquered by the British during
a trade war with the Dutch in Europe and North
America. New Netherland became New York.

During the early 1680s, another colony was established by William Penn on land that he called
Pennsylvania. Penn was a devout member of the Society
of Friends. These Protestants were known as Quakers
because they supposedly "quaked in the presence of
God." The Quakers ran their churches, known as
Quaker Meeting Houses, without clergy or ministers.
The Meeting Houses were simple wooden structures
where every Quaker was given an opportunity to speak.
Quakers believed that everyone was equal in the sight
of God. They were also opposed to killing another
human being, even during war. This meant that every
Quaker was a pacifist.

Penn's father, a famous admiral, had been a close
friend of King Charles II. He had lent the king money.
After the admiral died, the king paid off the debt by
granting William Penn a large tract of land in North
America. Penn wanted his colony to become a center for

Charles II granted William Penn a large piece of land in America.

Quakers. The Quakers had been persecuted for their beliefs in England. Thousands of them had been sent to prison. Penn also offered complete religious toleration to other colonists who were not Quakers. In addition, Penn envisioned a government based on a governor and a legislature elected by all male landowners, "where the laws rule, and the people are a party to those laws, and more than this is tyranny . . . or confusion."[13]

In 1682, Penn arrived in Pennsylvania. He purchased additional land from the local American Indians at fair prices.[14] The rich soil enabled the colonists to bring in large harvests of corn, wheat, and tobacco. Penn also established a new settlement at Philadelphia. During the eighteenth century, Philadelphia would become one of the most important cities in the British colonies.

Trade, Agriculture, and Slavery

During the eighteenth century, most colonial families in America lived on farms and plantations. However, rough roads and broad rivers connected the countryside to small cities along the Atlantic coast. These cities included Boston; New York; Philadelphia; and Newport, Rhode Island in the North, as well as Charles Town (now Charleston) in South Carolina. These cities became lively centers of trade and economic growth.

The Economy of the North

Over ninety percent of the colonial population lived in the countryside during much of the eighteenth century.[1] Family farms in the Northern colonies averaged between fifty and three hundred acres of land. These farms grew corn and wheat. Farmers had learned to grow Indian corn from the American Indians. Each seed was planted about six feet from the next, giving the corn plant plenty of room to leaf out and flourish. An estimated fifteen hundred corn plants could be harvested on each acre of land.[2]

Another food crop widely raised in the North was wheat. A small farm might produce as much as eighty to ninety bushels per year.[3] Much of the corn and wheat were then taken to nearby mills. Located along rivers, the mills were driven by waterwheels. A shaft running from the waterwheel was connected by gears to two millstones. The corn and wheat kernels were poured between the stones and ground into flour. Farmers also raised hogs as a source of meat. Hogs were fed and fattened on corn. Chickens provided fresh eggs, and sheep served as a source of wool that could be spun into clothing.

Many Northern farmers produced more food than their families required. According to historian Cathy Matson, a family needed only about forty-five bushels of wheat a year to feed themselves. This was approximately half what they produced.[4] They traded some of the extra grain to the local miller to grind their wheat into flour. Then the farmers sold the rest of the surplus to merchants. These merchants shipped the grain, corn, hogs and woolen cloth to cities, like New York, Boston, and Philadelphia. The merchants then imported goods from abroad and sold them to the colonists.

During the eighteenth century, trade worked in several different ways. Some of the surplus food was sold inside a colony, like New York or Massachusetts. But historians estimate that approximately ten percent was exported from North America.[5] Much of the food went to the islands of the Caribbean. On these islands, planters grew sugarcane, not food crops.

Sugar was a highly valued product in Europe for sweetening tea and coffee.

With the money they made selling farm produce to the Caribbean sugar islands, colonial merchants bought products in Europe. Philadelphia merchants, for example, brought back fine wines from Portugal. Among the leading Philadelphia merchants were Edward Shippen and Richard Willing. Their ships were regularly sailing back and forth to England. One of their advertisements read: "Lately imported from Bristol [England], in the Ship Jane Galley, likely Servants, Men Women and Boys, bred to most sorts of Business; fine white Salt, Glass-Bottles, and most Sorts of European Goods."[6]

New York merchant Gerard Beekman imported glass to the colonies from England, and brought in coffee and cocoa from the Netherlands. In New York, some merchants specialized in specific imported products. Jacobus van Zant was a cloth merchant, while John Watts brought in wine as well as molasses, a product made from sugarcane, that was used in making rum.[7]

Items from abroad were purchased by colonists of all classes. These included the wealthy as well as the lower classes, farmers as well as city people. According to historian T. H. Breen, more and more items were advertised in local newspapers. In the *Pennsylvania Gazette*, the number of ads rose from ten to four hundred per issue between 1733 and 1773. Shops carried larger and larger quantities of goods for sale to consumers. These included

Irish linens, lace, fine china dishware, carpets, silver watches, fancy buckles, and silver spoons.[8]

Many products were offered for sale by local merchants in towns, like Philadelphia. Store owners opened shops in part of their homes to sell their goods. In the same neighborhoods, artisans also offered their wares for sales. These artisans included fine silversmiths, jewelers, and goldsmiths. In Boston, a London jeweler named James Boyer opened a shop in 1723. Another artisan, William Goodwin, offered spectacles for sale in his shop. John Cowell combined his skills as a goldsmith and a coffee seller in his store.[9]

Northern Fur Trade

From the seventeenth century, merchants in Albany, New York, had carried on a brisk fur trade. They traded with the Iroquois. These Indians acquired furs from American Indians farther west. Beaver pelts were highly valued for making fur hats. Deerskins were made into leather shoes and clothing. Often the furs were traded for pots and pans, muskets, and rum. In the late 1740s, Swedish scientist Peter Kalm visited Albany, the center of the Northern fur trade. As Kalm wrote:

> Many people have assured me that the Indians are frequently cheated in disposing of their goods, especially when they are drunk, and that sometimes they do not get one half or even one tenth of the value of their goods. I have been a witness to several transactions of this kind.[10]

Among the most successful New York merchants in

The tomahawk above is not an authentic American Indian tomahawk. It is called a "trade tomahawk" and was actually made by the colonists. They made them so that they could trade them to the American Indians for beaver pelts, food, and other goods.

the fur trade was Cornelius Cuyler. According to one report in 1732, he sold "yearly here to our hatters above 3000 lbs. of Beaver."[11] In addition, Cuyler traded with the French colony of Canada. The French obtained furs from American Indians in return for kettles, guns, and other items. Cuyler's trade with French Canada was illegal because the French and British were often at war with each other. Nevertheless, British traders in Albany regularly broke the law. The Indians often preferred British trade items. They were good quality and less expensive than French items.

But trade did not remain inside the cities themselves. Colonial farmers took the money they made selling their produce to buy items for their homes. Some of these were sold in local stores that opened in small villages. Other items were brought along the roadways by peddlers. James Gray, for example, sold books throughout the New England countryside. Others sold products from their horsecarts that included "Mens [sic] wearing Apparel ... Coats, Breeches, Shoes, Buckles, Shirts, Neckcloaths [sic], and Gloves, ... also Salt, Nutmegs, ... Olives, Cinamon [sic], and several other sort of Goods."[12] In addition, farmers bought pewter dishes, knives, forks, and spoons. All of these were products that the small farmer could not produce for himself. It is easy to believe that colonial farmers and their families were self-sufficient—that they produced all that they needed on their farms and were totally independent. But the reality was far different.

Population of Colonial Cities by Year			
	1700	**1720**	**1742**
Boston	6,700	12,000	16,258
New York	5,000	7,000	11,000
Philadelphia	5,000	10,000	13,000
Newport	2,600	3,800	6,200
Charles Town	2,000	3,500	6,800[13]

Newport and the Slave Trade

Among the largest towns in the North was Newport, Rhode Island. The colony had relatively poor, rocky soil. As a result, there was not a large quantity of farm produce to be sold from Newport to other areas of the

The first slaves may have come to America as early as 1619. It was in this year that a Dutch ship delivered twenty Africans to Jamestown. It is unclear, however, whether the Africans were enslaved or were indentured servants.

world. Gradually, the Newport merchants turned to the slave trade during the eighteenth century. In this period, merchants in Newport and smaller coastal towns made more than nine hundred trips to the west coast of Africa to purchase enslaved Africans. According to one estimate, one hundred thousand Africans came to America in Rhode Island slave ships.[14]

The slavers traded rum for captives from local groups in West Africa. Many of these kingdoms or groups battled each other. They would frequently sell their captured enemies into slavery. Long lines of slaves were shackled together and brought to the coast. Here slave traders had set up holding pens called barracoons. Slaves were kept in these barracoons. They were chained together until enough of them had been collected for shipment to the New World.

Newport slavers sailed in small ships. As a result, they tried to pack as many slaves as possible below decks to make the voyage profitable. Men were put into one part of the ship's hold, while women were housed in another area. Often, the space was only two to three feet high, so the enslaved Africans could not stand. Instead, they had to lie on their sides. The voyage from Africa to the New World lasted as long as three months. The African slaves spent much of their time below decks. This voyage was known as the Middle Passage because it was the second, or middle, portion of a three-part trade, called the triangular trade because the shipping routes form a triangle on a map. (The first part was the shipment of rum from Rhode Island to be traded for slaves in Africa.)

Once the Newport slavers had reached the Caribbean, they sold the slaves for sugar and molasses. These products were transported to Rhode Island, in what was the third part of the triangular trade. There they became the ingredients in fine quality rum. The rum was then shipped to West Africa to trade for another shipment of slaves.

Slavery in the Colonies

In addition to Newport, a lucrative slave trade was carried on by other North American merchants. They

Witness to the Middle Passage

Alexander Falconbridge served on English slave ships during the eighteenth century. As he later explained, "The hardships and inconveniences suffered by the Negroes [an old term for Africans or African Americans, which is considered offensive today] during the passage are scarcely to be enumerated or conceived. They are far more violently affected by seasickness than Europeans. It frequently terminates in death, especially among the women."

Very little fresh air ever reached below decks, Falconbridge continued, "The fresh air being thus excluded, the Negroes rooms soon grown intolerable hot. The confined air, rendered noxious by the effluvia exhaled from their bodies and being repeatedly breathed, soon produces fevers . . . which generally carries off great numbers of them."[15] At various times of day the slaves were brought on deck for food and exercise. Ship captains tried to prevent too many slave deaths because their profit would be reduced. However, as many as 7.5 percent of the slaves died during the Middle Passage.[16]

operated out of Boston, New York, Philadelphia, Charles Town, and other smaller towns. Many of these slaves were brought to the American colonies. In the North, there were approximately thirty thousand slaves by 1750.[17] They made up about 5 to 10 percent of the population. Most of the slaves were found in cities, where they worked in shipbuilding or assisted local artisans. Others were owned by wealthy merchants who kept slaves as household servants. In the countryside, slaves also worked on farms.

The majority of slaves lived in the Southern colonies. There they were concentrated on large plantations. Most small farmers did not own slaves. The first Africans had arrived in Virginia in 1619. They were purchased by John Rolfe to work on his tobacco plantation. Historians are not certain whether these Africans were slaves or indentured servants. By the middle of the seventeenth century, however, the number of slaves had increased. Fewer indentured servants were arriving from England where economic conditions had improved and there was more work. In addition, planters began to prefer slaves because they did not need to be released after seven years. They were forced to work on a plantation for life. As historian Ira Berlin wrote, about 1668, the population of indentured servants was five times the slave population in much of the Chesapeake area of Virginia. By 1700, the numbers were just the opposite.[18]

Virginia had a slave population of sixteen thousand in 1700. Fifty years later, the population had grown to one hundred and seven thousand. During the same period, the slave population had grown from three thousand to forty three thousand in Maryland. This colony had been founded in the 1630s. In South Carolina, founded thirty years later, the number of slaves had also grown. The slave population there reached thirty-nine thousand by 1750. In fact, there were more African Americans living in South Carolina than European settlers. In all, more than two hundred thousand African-American slaves lived in the South.[19]

Slaves were forced to work no matter what the conditions. They were slaves for life and were often treated harshly by their owners.

Some Northern colonists were strongly opposed to

slavery. Quakers, for example, spoke out against slavery. During the 1750s, they refused to admit any members who participated in the slave trade. They also urged all Quakers who held slaves to free them immediately.

Slavery and the Southern Economy

During the eighteenth century, slaves became a large part of the Southern economy. They worked on the tobacco plantations of Virginia and Maryland as well as the rice plantations of South Carolina. According to historian Richard Middleton, tobacco was the most important crop in North America. Production almost tripled between 1700 and 1760, making up forty-five percent of all exports from the colonies to England.[20] When tobacco was grown on a plantation, the plant took many nutrients from the soil. As a result, tobacco could not continue to be produced after a few years. Therefore, Southern farmers and plantation owners began growing wheat during the mid-eighteenth century. The price of tobacco regularly went up and down in England. Wheat gave the Southern farmers another steadier source of income. Meanwhile, Southern planters also began to buy up more and more land on the frontier. Here, they established new tobacco plantations.

The demands of growing tobacco meant that planters wanted more and more slaves in order to make a large profit. Slavers regularly stopped at plantations along the Chesapeake Bay. Other slaves were auctioned off at slave markets inside the city to work on the Carolina rice plantations.

Slaves were often sold from one owner to another. Sometimes they were even separated from family in this way.

Many slaves came from Africa with direct experience growing rice, which flourished in a hot climate. Therefore, they proved invaluable to rice planters who needed workers to plant the fields, irrigate them, and harvest the rice. By 1740, about forty million pounds of rice were exported from South Carolina each year.[21] During the mid-eighteenth century, South Carolina introduced another crop, indigo. It was first grown by Eliza Pinckney at her plantation, Wappoo. The indigo plant produced a purple dye, highly prized in Europe. Indigo was used for clothing, especially among royalty who wore lavish purple robes.

Unlike the Northern colonies, there were few sizable towns in the South, except Charles Town. As a result, planters often turned their own plantations into small towns. Ships from England arrived at plantation wharves bringing necessary farm implements and other supplies for the plantation. But many other items were produced on the plantation itself. Slaves were trained to do a variety of jobs, in addition to working in the fields. Virginian George Mason grew up on a plantation where he said his father "had among his slaves carpenters, coopers [barrel makers], sawyers, blacksmiths, tanners . . . shoemakers, spinners, weavers and knitters, and even a distiller."[22]

In the South, white owners and black slaves formed a unique society. Nothing like it existed in England, where there was no slavery. Indeed, Southern aristocrats lived like no other people in North America.

Colonial Society

During the eighteenth century, the owners of large plantations in South Carolina were the wealthiest men in North America. In other colonies, there were also well-to-do landowners and merchants who wore magnificent clothing and lived in fine mansions. They were considered gentlemen and set apart from other colonials. A rung below the wealthy lived the majority of the colonists. They were called the middling sort or middle class. The middling sort included small farmers, shop owners, and skilled tradesmen. At the bottom of society were slaves and the unemployed.

Southern Aristocrats

Henry Middleton was among the richest men in South Carolina. He owned eight hundred slaves. They worked on his fifty-thousand-acre plantation, called Middleton Hall. Joseph Wragg grew rich as a slaver. Then he invested in plantations and became a successful planter. These men and their friends ruled Carolina society. Their homes gleamed with gilt-edged mirrors, beautiful chandeliers, the finest silver, and highly polished furniture imported from England.

When they were not to be found on their large estates, the plantation owners lived in magnificent town-houses. These were located in the best sections of Charles Town. African or African-American servants opened the doors as visitors entered the houses to attend lavish dinners. Coachmen drove the plantation owners and their wives in shiny carriages to fancy-dress balls given in Charles Town.

Charles Town was the chief city of the South. It boasted theaters, race tracks, and fine taverns where the wealthy gathered to enjoy themselves. In Charles Town, the wealthy regularly attended plays at the Queen Street Theater that had come directly from the London stage.[1]

A Slave Society

The planters and their families lived at the top of the social pyramid. Beneath them were hundreds of farmers, merchants, and shopkeepers. They lived in much smaller houses. However, many of them had at least one servant, usually an African American. This servant cleaned the house, cooked meals, and did the washing.

The South was a society built on slavery. The life of the slaves was often far different from the lifestyle of the people they were forced to serve. Many slaves lived on the large plantations. On the plantations, the slaves were kept under control by what historian Ira Berlin has called "raw power." Planters did not hesitate to use "the rod, the lash, the branding iron, and the fist with increased regularity" when the slaves disobeyed.[2] William Byrd owned a vast estate in Virginia called Westover where he employed many slaves. In his diary, Byrd recorded that he regularly beat his slaves. Byrd wrote that on February 8, 1709, "Jenny and Eugene were whipped." On December 1, 1709, "Eugene was whipped again for [wetting] in bed." February 27, 1711, "In the evening my wife and

This medallion shows how American slaves were sometimes confined in shackles.

little Jenny [a slave] had a great quarrel in which my wife got the worst but at last by the help of the family Jenny was overcome and soundly whipped."[3]

To back up the power of the plantation owners, Southern colonies passed a series of slave codes. According to these codes, slaves were prohibited from leaving their plantations without a written pass. They were also forbidden to carry weapons. They could not meet in large groups away from the plantation. These laws were designed to prevent slave revolts.

However, the slave codes also required the plantation owners to properly feed and clothe the slaves. Owners were also expected to provide slaves with living quarters. Some plantation owners prided themselves on how well they cared for their slaves. But in reality many slaves were underfed and poorly clothed. The slave quarters, where the slaves lived, often was a ramshackle area. Slave families lived in small, one-room cabins. The cabins were brutally hot in summer and very cold in winter.

Most African-American men and women on the plantations married and had families. These children were raised not only by their parents, but also by a large extended family of aunts, uncles, and grandparents. Sometimes these extended families included slaves living on other plantations. Slaves might be sold off by their owners to neighboring plantations. Some slaves never saw their families again. If they were fortunate, however, slaves were permitted to travel on weekends and visit relatives.

Society in the Northern Colonies

There were far fewer slaves in the North, but they were mistreated by their owners just like those in the South. In 1735, John van Zandt used a whip to beat his slave so badly that he died. However, van Zandt was acquitted by a jury that decided the whipping "was not the Cause of his Death, but that it was by the Visitation of God." In 1741, the so-called "Negro Conspiracy" occurred in New York. Residents of the city were convinced that African Americans were behind a rash of robberies. No evidence, however, tied them to the crimes. Nevertheless, the militia arrested many innocent slaves. Thirteen were burned at the stake and eight others were hanged.[4]

In cities like New York, Boston, and Philadelphia, crime was a continuing problem. Many of these crimes were committed by the poor. In Philadelphia, riots among the poor broke out from 1741 to 1742. Meanwhile, some communities were trying to provide help for their poorer residents. Local churches made contributions to provide food and clothing for the poor. Boston and New York established almshouses where the poor lived and worked. According to one estimate, 25 percent of

Slave Revolts

In 1712, a slave revolt broke out in New York. On April 6, Cuffee, a slave, and a group of African Americans torched a house in the city and planned to go to other houses and murder the occupants. But the slaves were captured and later executed. In 1739, a slave revolt broke out near Charles Town at Stono River. About fifty settlers were killed before the revolt was finally put down by the colonial militia.

people lived in poverty in Boston during the 1740s. Outside the cities, many of the poor worked as tenant farmers on someone else's land. However, many of these people saved their money and acquired their own land. In the countryside, the poverty level was probably about 5 percent.[5]

The majority of people in the North were middle-class farmers, shopkeepers, or artisans. Many of them hoped to eventually become members of the upper class. A few finally achieved their goal.

The well-to-do in New York, Philadelphia, and Boston lived much as the wealthy planters did in Charles Town. They built magnificent homes. These homes were filled with expensive furniture and cleaned

Philadelphia quickly grew into a thriving city and port.

Benjamin Franklin—a Man on the Rise

The American colonies offered many people an opportunity to rise up in the world. Perhaps the most famous example was Benjamin Franklin. Born in Boston in 1706, Franklin was one of seventeen children. His father was a struggling candlemaker. During the 1700s, many children were sent out by their parents to become apprentices. They were required to work without pay for their masters until the age of twenty-one. In return, they learned a trade from their masters, who might be carpenters or shoemakers. These masters also gave them food and clothing.

Franklin was apprenticed to his older brother James, the publisher of the *New England Courant*. However, Benjamin and his brother did not get along well. James beat Benjamin regularly. In 1723, the younger Franklin left for New York and later Philadelphia. As Franklin wrote, James' "harsh and tyrannical treatment of me [was] a means of impressing me with that aversion to arbitrary power that has stuck to me through my whole life."[6]

In the late 1720s, Franklin opened his own printing business. During the 1730s, he became the highly successful publisher of *The Pennsylvania Gazette*. He also published *Poor Richard's Almanack*. It was one of the most widely read publications in the American colonies, helping to make Franklin famous. In it, he published memorable quotations such as "A penny saved is a penny earned" and "Early to bed, early to rise makes a man healthy, wealthy, and wise." He firmly believed that hard work helped any man improve himself.

Franklin retired from the publishing business in 1748. Afterward, he experimented with electricity and invented the lightning rod. This work made Franklin famous across Europe. Very ambitious and eager to serve his colony, Franklin also became one of the leading politicians in Pennsylvania. By the end of his life he was against slavery and was named president of the first antislavery society in America.

by live-in servants. Some Philadelphia merchants could even afford to have their portraits painted by noted artists, such as Robert Feke and Gustavus Hesselius. Other members of the upper class in Philadelphia had enough leisure time to take music lessons. They also attended concerts at the Musick Club and read books. By the middle of the eighteenth century, Philadelphia had more bookstores than any other community in North America.[7]

Immigrants to America

The American colonies seemed to be a land of opportunity to many people who lived in Europe. Among them were the Scots. Scottish farmers and artisans lived not only in Scotland but also in Northern Ireland. Both of these regions were, like England, part of Great Britain. In Ireland, they were known as the Scots-Irish. A poor economy caused one hundred and forty-five thousand of them to immigrate to the American colonies during the eighteenth century. Similar conditions led to the immigration of over one hundred thousand people from Germany.[8] As the first streams of immigrants arrived in America, they often wrote to others, urging them to follow.

Many of the new settlers went to Pennsylvania, a colony that supported religious toleration. They often arrived in Philadelphia, and then moved to the frontier where land was cheap. Others went to Virginia and the Carolinas. Scratching out farms from the wilderness and building new homes was hard work.

But many settlers seemed satisfied that they had come to America. On the frontier, they could enjoy liberty of conscience. They could worship as they chose and say what they wanted without fear of being arrested.

Scratching out farms from the wilderness and building new homes was hard work.

These freedoms were not available in much of Europe. As one new settler put it, "Liberty of conscience [was the] chief virtue of this land, and on this store I do not repent my immigration. But for this freedom, I think this country would not improve so rapidly."[9]

Colonial Families

Frequently, entire families came from Europe to the American colonies. Along the frontier, men and women often worked side by side in the fields. Here they established new lives for themselves. But, as historian Richard Middleton has written, once the farms were established, women went back to "their more traditional household occupations."[10]

Throughout most of colonial America, women found themselves in a subordinate role to their husbands. This was the same situation that existed in Europe. Women took care of the home, while men worked as artisans, merchants, and shopkeepers. There were exceptions. Some women spun cloth at home that they sold in nearby towns. A few women in

Georgia

In 1733, a group of more than one hundred settlers led by Colonel James Oglethorpe established a settlement on the coast of Georgia. It was located on the site of present-day Savannah. "I have laid out a town, opposite to which is an island of very rich pasturage, which I think should be kept for . . . cattle," Oglethorpe wrote. "For about six miles up into the country the landscape is very agreeable, the stream being wide and bordered with high woods on both sides."[11]

The colony was named after Britain's King George II.

Georgia was originally designed as a refuge for debtors who were about to be thrown into prison. Oglethorpe was a member of the British Parliament. He had led an effort to improve the lot of men and women who were jailed because they could not pay their debts. Parliament agreed to pay for the cost of transporting the poor to Georgia.

While few debtors chose to come to North America, other settlers did travel to the new colony. Georgia became another example of religious toleration, welcoming Protestants of many faiths. These included Puritans and Quakers. Scottish settlers also moved to Georgia and established homesteads on the frontier.

At first the colony banned slavery. Each settler received a small plot of land and raised hemp, essential for ropes on English ships. They also grew flax, a plant from which linen was made. However, some of the Georgia settlers became wealthier. They demanded the right to have larger farms and employ slaves. Eventually, slaves were transported to Georgia where they worked on large plantations.

cities ran small shops together with their husbands. Some women also ran inns and grocery stores. Other women worked as midwives, helping other women to deliver their babies.

By and large, a woman's role in colonial America was to marry and raise a family. The overwhelming

This spinning wheel was used in colonial times to make yarn.

majority of women married. Indeed, single women were considered strange and called "old maids." Men and women usually married in their early twenties, at least among the middle and upper classes. They lived in nuclear families, consisting of parents and children. During the first year of life, children were wrapped in swaddling clothes. These were strips of linen wrapped tightly around a baby's body to insure that his or her back remained straight. Colonial parents also tried to teach a child to walk upright as quickly as possible.

About the age of six, children began helping their parents with household chores. While girls remained at home, boys were often sent out to become apprentices. Among the wealthy, boys were tutored at home or sent to school. Some even went to colleges. These included Yale in New Haven, Connecticut, and Harvard, in Cambridge, Massachusetts.

Girls, however, were given very little education. Most parents believed that education was wasted on girls who were expected to marry and run households. Their brothers, however, were destined for much larger roles. Perhaps the most important was governing the colonies.

Colonial Government

Colonial government operated at several different levels. Most colonists only came into contact with local government, in their towns or counties. But in each colonial capital sat a governor, his council of advisors, and a legislature. They made laws for the entire colony. Finally, each colony was part of the British Empire. The empire was governed by the ministers of the king and the British parliament.

Local Government

In Virginia and other parts of the South, the main unit of local government was called a vestry. The vestry also ran the local Anglican church. Virginia had an established church. That is, the Anglican churches were supported by local taxes. Members of the vestry, who were usually well-to-do planters and merchants, were in charge of levying taxes to support the local church parishes. They also paid the clergyman in each parish. He received sixteen thousand pounds of tobacco each year.[1] He sold the tobacco to obtain his income. Each vestry was in charge of caring for the local poor as well as orphaned children. The vestry also took responsibility for making sure that colonists who were guilty of small crimes, like public drunkenness, were brought before local judges for trial.

Many well-to-do planters began their government service on the vestries. They might also serve as judges in the county courts. The counties were large units of government that contained a collection of parishes. Virginia planters also ran for election to the Virginia legislature. This was the House of Burgesses, located in the colonial capital, Williamsburg. Running for a seat in the House of Burgesses was expensive. Candidates courted local voters by putting on all kinds of parties, even barbecues. Only the wealthy could usually afford such expenditures. Some of these men were also appointed by the governor as members of his council. As historian Daniel Boorstin has written, twenty-three well-to-do families in Virginia provided almost two-thirds of the governor's councillors during most of the eighteenth century.[2]

The governors in the Southern colonies were generally appointed by the English government in London. In some cases, the governor was an English nobleman who never traveled to the colonies. Instead he appointed a lieutenant governor to run the government for him.

In the mid-Atlantic colonies and in New England, provincial government varied. In Pennsylvania, the governor was selected by a member of the Penn family. In Connecticut and Rhode Island, local voters selected the governors. But in most colonies, the governor was appointed by the British government. Throughout

North America, governors had the power to make important appointments, like judges of the provincial courts. However, the colonial legislatures determined how much money should be spent on the defense of the colony. The legislature also paid the governor. This gave the legislators enormous power to control political decisions.

Local government varied in the Northern colonies. Some areas of the mid-Atlantic colonies had counties, but other sections had town government. Town governments also existed throughout New England. The towns were run by elected officials called selectmen. They were in charge of levying taxes on property owners to pay for local services. These included paving roads. In Boston, for example, the town government hired residents to pave the roads. The pavement consisted of gravel or cobblestones.[3]

Public safety was another responsibility of local government. In New York, a town was governed by a mayor and his councillors. The council ordered that

Perhaps the biggest problem confronting large towns was fire.

a local watch should be hired to patrol the streets throughout the night to prevent crime. Towns also began putting up streetlights. These helped residents make their way home at night and discouraged criminals from hiding in the darkness.

Perhaps the biggest problem confronting large towns was fire. Most houses were made of wood. A fire that broke out in one house could rapidly sweep through an entire community. In 1740, Charles Town suffered a terrible fire that wiped out a large part of the city's wooden houses. Boston tried to prevent a similar occurrence. The local government ordered that all new buildings should be constructed of brick. The city also appointed chimney inspectors to make sure that each chimney was properly cleaned. Hot embers from fireplaces could create fires in the chimneys and burn down houses.

Large cities, such as New York, also purchased fire engines. These were water pumps drawn by horses and manned by volunteer firemen. In 1736, Benjamin Franklin founded a volunteer fire department in Philadelphia. It was called the Union Fire Company. But volunteers and early fire engines were usually unable to prevent a house from burning to the ground. Instead, the volunteers rushed into the building with salvage bags. They tried to save only the homeowner's valuables. Among these was the bed, which was disassembled and removed from the house. To help deal with fire loss, Franklin began the "Philadelphia Contributorship" in 1740. This was an early type of insurance company.

The British Empire

The American colonies were part of the far-flung British Empire. It included not only North America,

James De Lancey

In the American colonies, only male property owners could vote, an estimated 50 percent of the population.[4] The largest property owners usually ran the government. In New York, one of the largest landowners was James De Lancey. Born in 1703, De Lancey was the son of a successful merchant, Stephen De Lancey, and Anne van Cortlandt. Her family was among the wealthiest Dutch landowners in the colony. De Lancey went to London in 1723 to receive a law degree. Upon returning to New York, he married Ann Heathcote. She was the daughter of a leading colonial politician.

During the 1730s, De Lancey served on the governor's council and as a member of the colonial Supreme Court. He also had many friends and political allies in the New York assembly. Finally, during most of the 1750s, De Lancey served as acting governor of New York. He was among the most powerful politicians in colonial America until his death in 1760.

but also colonies in the Caribbean and India. The British government believed that the colonies existed for the benefit of the mother country. This theory was known as mercantilism. According to mercantilism, the colonies provided markets for English goods. The colonies also produced raw materials, such as tobacco and sugar, for the English market.

During the seventeenth and eighteenth centuries the English parliament passed a series of laws known as the Navigation Acts. These acts specified that the North American colonies were required to sell products, such as tobacco, only to England. Even if they could get a better price for tobacco in another European country, the colonists were not permitted to sell it there. The Navigation Acts also required that all colonial goods must be shipped in English ships. Since the colonists were part of the British Empire, they could ship products such as corn to the Caribbean or rum to Africa in return for slaves. Meanwhile, the British navy, the most powerful in the world, protected colonial merchants from attack. English taxpayers supported the navy to provide security for colonial merchants and defense for the British colonies.

In many parts of the world, the British Empire was challenged by France. In North America, the French controlled a large empire in Canada, known as New France. The capital of New France, Quebec, was located on the St. Lawrence River. Another large town on the St. Lawrence was Montreal. The French had also established important trading posts along the Great Lakes, down the Mississippi River, and in Louisiana. From these posts, French traders developed strong relationships with local American Indians.

During the seventeenth and early eighteenth centuries, Britain and France had battled against each other in a series of bloody wars in North America. French troops as well as their American Indian allies made regular raids against British colonial towns. In 1704, for example, Deerfield, Massachusetts, was attacked and almost destroyed by the French. In 1713, however, Britain and France concluded a peace agreement. For the next thirty years, peace reigned and commerce flourished. British merchants did not need to fear possible attack from French warships.

Battle for Victory

In 1744, war between France and Britain broke out again. Known as King George's War in North America, it was part of a larger conflict that had spread across Europe. In 1745, the American colonists launched an attack on Louisburg. This was a French fortress on Cape Breton Island that guarded the mouth of the St. Lawrence River. The expedition was organized by Governor William Shirley of Massachusetts. It included New England ships and soldiers as well as artillery and supplies from the mid-Atlantic colonies. After a siege lasting six weeks, the fortress finally surrendered in June 1745. This important battle proved that the colonies could work together and win a great military victory. However, according to the terms of the peace treaty signed in 1748, Louisburg was returned to France.

Following the end of King George's War, the conflict between Britain and France moved to the Ohio Valley. Both France and Britain claimed the valley as part of their empires. France regarded the area as an important link between its colonies in Canada and the Mississippi River. The British saw the Ohio Valley as an important area to promote trade with American Indians. British settlers also wanted to establish new farms and communities there.

In 1749, a Pennsylvania trader named George Croghan established an important trading post at Pickawillany. This was a Miami Indian village in the Ohio Valley. Croghan and other traders attracted many Indians who came to Pickawillany to purchase British goods. During the same year, a group of Virginia investors, known as the Ohio Company, established a post at Wills Creek. This was located in the present-day state of Maryland. They surveyed the surrounding area, hoping to attract American settlers to the Ohio Valley.

However, the French were not prepared to lose control of the valley. Nor could they afford to give up the alliances of major Indian tribes like the Miami and Delaware who lived there. In 1752, a small French and Indian army led by Charles-Michel Mouet de Langlade struck Pickawillany. Surprising the Indians and traders, the French burned the town and killed many of its inhabitants. They removed the heart of one trader and ate it. Then they boiled the body of the dead Miami chief, Memeskia, and ate him, too.[5] The English traders were so frightened that they immediately left the area. In 1753, the French followed up on the destruction of Pickawillany. They sent a detachment of soldiers to establish a series of forts from Lake Erie to the Allegheny River. France intended to control the entire Ohio Valley.

However, Robert Dinwiddie, the lieutenant governor of Virginia, had other ideas. Late in 1753, Dinwiddie dispatched a young major in the colonial militia, George Washington, to the Ohio Valley. Along with six other men, Washington was to travel to Fort Le Boeuf. This was one of the French forts established south of Lake Erie. Trudging through deep snow and ice, the six-foot-four-inch-tall Washington finally reached Fort Le Boeuf. He delivered a letter from Lieutenant Governor Dinwiddie to the French commander. Since the lands of the Ohio, Dinwiddie wrote, were "known to be the property of the Crown of Great Britain . . . it is a matter of equal concern and surprise to me, to hear that a body of French forces are erecting fortresses and making settlements . . . within his Majesty's dominions."[6] However, the French were not impressed with Dinwiddie's letter. They sent

In a 1754 article, Benjamin Franklin wrote about the need for a colonial union. It was necessary, he said, to defend against the French and to deal with the Indians. With the article was the picture of a snake cut into pieces, which represented the colonies. Under it, were the words "Join or Die."

Washington back to Virginia. He carried a letter, saying that the Ohio Valley belonged to the king of France.

Early in 1754, Dinwiddie and the Virginia legislature ordered Washington to enlist a force of two hundred men and return to the Ohio Valley. Meanwhile, Virginia also began building a small fort at the fork of the Ohio and Allegheny rivers. As the fort was being constructed, however, a large force of French soldiers appeared along the river. They ordered the small company of Virginians to abandon their post. The French replaced the fort with a much larger one. It was called Fort Du Quesne, in honor of the Marquis Du Quesne, governor-general of Canada.

While the French were taking charge of the fork of the Ohio, Washington and his men had established a small outpost to the east. Known as Fort Necessity, it was a wooden stockade. Fort Necessity was located at the Great Meadows, in present-day western Pennsylvania. On May 28, 1754, Washington intercepted a small French force of thirty-five men. They had been sent to scout Fort Necessity. Some of the French scouts were killed and the rest captured. Late in June, a much larger French force of six hundred men marched against Washington's outpost. The French occupied a position in the surrounding hills. Then they fired down on the colonial troops inside Fort Necessity. Washington was finally forced to surrender. However, the French allowed him to retreat with his men to Virginia.

The French and Indian War

George Washington's small battles in the Ohio Valley touched off a major conflict between France and Britain. The war spread across Europe, India, and the Caribbean. In Europe, it was called the Seven Years' War. But in North America the conflict was known as the French and Indian War. Meanwhile, the British government had ordered that the colonies meet together to develop a joint plan of defense. In July 1754, colonial delegates met in Albany, New York. The Albany Congress was hosted by acting governor James De Lancey. Among the delegates was Benjamin Franklin from Pennsylvania. Franklin proposed that the colonies create a union, known as the Albany Plan of Union. The unified government would have its own assembly to raise taxes. It would also have an executive branch to recruit an army.

However, the colonists were far too divided to agree on a common policy. New York wanted assistance in building forts to defend against a French invasion from Canada. But the other colonial legislatures would not contribute any money. The colonies also could not agree on which of them should take over American Indian lands in the Ohio Valley. As a result, there was no common defense policy.

Meanwhile, the British government had sent a contingent of troops to North America. It was commanded by General Edward Braddock. General Braddock intended to lead an attack on Fort Du Quesne. Once the fort fell, Braddock could take back control of the Ohio Valley from France.

Braddock almost succeeded. By July 1755, his army of about twenty-two hundred men was only a few miles from the French fort. They had been joined by New York and Virginia militias that had helped carve a road through the wilderness. As the army marched through the woods on the early afternoon of July 9, they suddenly saw American Indian warriors and French soldiers ahead of them. The British troops stopped and fired, killing several of the enemy. The rest of the enemy immediately spread out into the woods.

From these positions, the enemy began firing on the

General Braddock was defeated easily by French and American Indian Forces. The British were not used to the fighting style that their enemies used. The French and Indians hid behind trees and other cover. The British were used to the old style of fighting where two armies lined up across from one another in the open and charged.

British. Instead of taking cover behind the trees, the British soldiers were trained to stay in formation in the open and fire. As a result, they became sitting ducks for the French and Indians, who picked off the British from the woods. As one British soldier put it, "If we saw of them five or six at one time [it] was a great sight and they Either on their Bellies or Behind trees or Running from one tree to another almost by the ground."[7] Although General Braddock tried to rally his troops, it was no use. Braddock himself was eventually hit, and his army began to run from the battlefield. The Battle of the Wilderness, also known as Braddock's Defeat, became a disaster. Washington, who accompanied Braddock into the battle, was fortunate not to have been wounded. He helped the survivors make their way back from the frontier.

Washington was put in charge of raising a militia to guard the Virginia frontier. But there was little he could do to stop the French and their American Indian allies. They swooped down on small settlements, burning homes and killing settlers.

In the North, the military situation was not much better. Massachusetts, New York, and other colonies tried to defend their settlers. However, the French seemed too powerful. In 1756, a new British commander took charge in North America. John Campbell, Lord Loudoun, believed that his position as commander-in-chief gave him the power to order colonial governors and legislatures to do as he wished. He wanted the colonies to appropriate money to raise more troops. He also ordered them to quarter his soldiers in colonial homes. The legislatures refused to yield to Lord Loudoun. They regarded their control of the purse to be a liberty that could not be taken away. In addition, they believed that being forced to quarter British troops violated their rights as British citizens.

Lord Loudoun and the colonial governments strongly disagreed with each other. Meanwhile, the French sailed across Lake Ontario in western New York. French troops under the command of Marquis de Montcalm besieged the important British post at Fort Oswego. The fort fell in August 1756 to a combined force of French and Indians.

In July 1757, a French army of six thousand troops accompanied by two thousand Indians sailed down

George Washington (left, on horse) proved his military ability during the French and Indian War.

Lake George in central New York. Their destination was the British outpost at the foot of the lake, Fort William Henry. The main British army had been sent to attack Louisburg. Therefore, Fort William Henry was poorly defended. There was only a small force of colonial troops from New York, New Jersey, Massachusetts, and New Hampshire. They proved no match for the French. The French army under Montcalm had powerful artillery. Fort William Henry surrendered on August 9.

The situation for the British colonists looked terrible. Nevertheless, in London the tide of war was actually turning. A new prime minister, William Pitt, had conceived a bold plan for defeating the French. Unlike Lord Loudoun, Pitt also realized that the rights of the colonials had to be protected. He recognized that British generals were not superior to colonial governors and legislatures. Nor could they force colonials to quarter troops in their homes. In addition, Pitt offered to provide more money from London to pay colonial troops to fight the war.

In 1758, many additional colonial soldiers signed up to join the new British offensive. At the same time, the British navy was preventing important supplies and French troops from reaching Canada. In June, the British launched a successful attack on Louisburg. Meanwhile, a colonial officer, John Bradstreet, led an army of about three thousand troops from New York and New England. Their target was the French post at

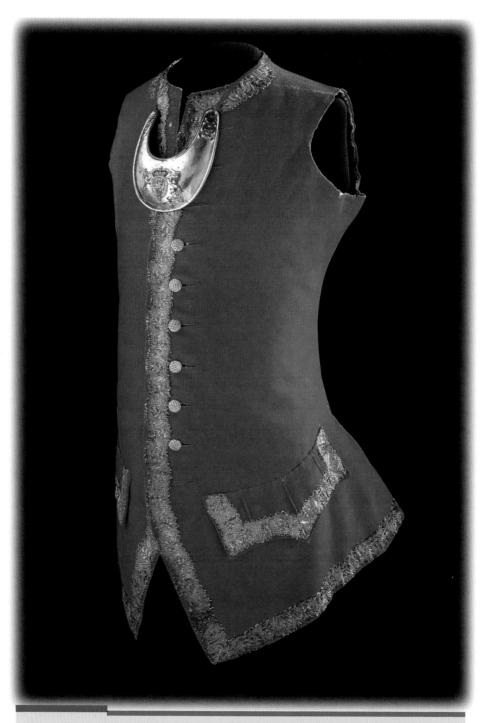

This uniform waistcoat was worn by Lieutenant Colonel Adam Stephen. Stephen was George Washington's second-in-command during the French and Indian War.

Fort Frontenac, on Lake Ontario. In August, they besieged the fort and captured it.

Farther south, colonial troops also participated in the British expedition against Fort Du Quesne. Partway through the campaign, the American Indians in the Ohio Valley switched their allegiance. They began to support the British. As a result, the French blew up Fort Du Quesne in November and fled northward. In 1759, English troops swept into Canada, capturing Quebec and, the following year, Montreal.

As a result of the French and Indian War, England had taken control of a huge empire. But the war had also played an important role in the development of the American colonies. Colonists from different parts of North America had fought together during the campaigns of the war. They had learned how to cooperate and temporarily put aside regional differences. Colonial soldiers learned guerrilla tactics from the American Indians. This involved quick attacks on forces, then retreating before the enemy could regroup. The colonists discovered that they could be just as successful in battle as the British regular troops. Leaders like George Washington had been tested in the heat of battle. Meanwhile, colonial political leaders had been forced to defend their liberties. They were prepared to stand up to any British general to protect what they believed were their rights as British citizens. These experiences would play a critical part in events over the next two decades.

The Coming of Independence

The conquest of Quebec and Montreal led to huge celebrations in Boston, Philadelphia, and New York. American colonists were pleased to be part of the victorious British Empire. They were also proud to have contributed to such a great triumph. Benjamin Franklin said, "I am a BRITON." A New England clergyman added: "Now commences the Era of our quiet Enjoyment of those Liberties, which our Fathers purchased with the Toil of their whole Lives."[1]

The Aftermath of War

According to the Peace of 1763, England received Canada from France and all French territory east of the Mississippi River. After conquering this huge empire, the British faced the problem of governing it. The war had cost the British government many millions of dollars. In fact, Britain had piled up a huge debt, maintaining an army and navy around the world. The French were mostly gone. Therefore, the English commander-in-chief, Jeffrey Amherst, decided he could save some money in his dealings with the Indians. The British had been accustomed to giving the American Indians lavish presents. These helped to assure their support against the French. After the war ended, Amherst decided to cut off most of these gifts. As the commander-in-chief wrote, "Services must be rewarded; it has ever been a maxim with me; but as to purchasing the good behavior either of Indians, or any Others, [that] is what I do not understand; when men of what race soever behave ill, they must be punished but not bribed. . . ."[2]

As Amherst made this decision, the American Indians had become increasingly angry over the results of the war. Many had been allied with the French and were saddened by their defeat. The British victory had also opened up the Ohio Valley to settlement by American colonists. They began to travel down Braddock's road, built in 1755. The colonists established new farms on the frontier. Speculators, such as the Ohio Company, also reappeared in the Ohio Valley to buy and sell land. In April 1763, an American Indian revolt broke out along the frontier. The uprising was directed by the Ottawa chief, Pontiac. Under his leadership, various Indians joined together. They captured several British outposts and laid siege to others.

The British army struggled to defeat the uprising. Meanwhile, Parliament issued the Proclamation of 1763. This order closed the frontier west of the Appalachian Mountains. The colonists were prohibited from buying Indian lands without the permission of the British government. With this proclamation, the British hoped to help achieve peace on the frontier. They also expected to lower the cost of defending it against Indian uprisings. But the new proclamation disappointed many American colonists. They had seen the victory in the French and Indian War as an opportunity to move westward.

Many British political leaders were angry with the colonists.

Meanwhile, the British were not only trying to reduce military expenses but also to increase revenues. Many British political leaders were angry with the colonists. Colonial smuggling had continued during the recent war. Newport merchants, for example, were purchasing rum illegally from the French sugar islands in the Caribbean. In 1764, Parliament passed the Sugar Act. This act strictly enforced laws against smuggling. New courts were established to try any merchants who violated the Sugar Act. In addition, the act put new taxes on a favorite colonial drink, Madeira wine. Madeira was imported from Portugal. In the past, it had been imported without duties (import taxes).

These new taxes were imposed at a difficult time. The American colonies were struggling through a serious economic depression. Many merchants had supplied food, clothing, and other goods to the British army and navy during the war. Colonial farmers had also prospered because there was a ready market for their surplus crops. After the war, the demand for these products greatly declined. The British army was demobilized and reduced in size.

In Boston, the level of poverty grew. By 1764, the city was spending more than double what had been spent a decade earlier to support the poor. Virginia planters suffered, too. After the war, the price of tobacco fell. George Washington owned a large estate at Mt. Vernon. He found himself experiencing serious financial problems. To deal with the situation, he began growing wheat and trying to buy and sell land.[3]

In Boston, a young lawyer named James Otis, Jr., published an influential pamphlet in 1764. It was titled *The Rights of the British Colonies Asserted and Proved*. Otis argued that Parliament had no right to tax British citizens unless they had elected representatives to take part in the parliamentary debate. Otis pointed out that he was asking for no more than the same rights that people enjoyed in Britain.

The Stamp Act Crisis

In addition to the Sugar Act, Parliament announced its plan to pass a Stamp Act in 1765. The act called for a tax on anything that required the use of paper. This included court documents, newspapers, almanacs, and playing cards. Stamps also had to be put on papers filed by ship captains entering colonial harbors. As Benjamin Franklin—who was visiting Britain at the time—put it, the new tax "will affect the Printers more than anybody."[4] However, Franklin was prepared to accept the tax because it was not too high.

Many other colonists did not share Franklin's opinion. Protests rapidly began to break out across

This stamp was used by an American colonist. Colonists were required by British law to buy the stamp for certain items. Many colonists felt that this was unfair.

the colonies. In Virginia, a young member of the House of Burgesses, Patrick Henry, spoke out against the Stamp Act. He introduced a series of resolutions, called the Virginia Resolves. Among them was the fifth resolve, stating that "the General Assembly of this Colony have the *only and sole exclusive* Right and Power to lay Taxes and Impositions upon the Inhabitants of this Colony . . ."[5] Henry and many others believed that the colonial assemblies would lose all their power if they lost their control over taxes. This resolve was never passed by the House of Burgesses. However, it was printed in newspapers up and down the Atlantic seaboard.

Meanwhile protests broke out in towns and cities throughout the colonies. In Boston, a group of merchants and artisans, known as the Loyal Nine, helped organize mass demonstrations. Andrew Oliver, who had been appointed to collect the revenues from the stamp tax, was forced to give up his position. But the demonstrators were not satisfied. They broke into the home of Lieutenant Governor Thomas Hutchinson. He was a

Samuel Adams

Samuel Adams was among the most effective protest leaders speaking out against the Stamp Act. Born in 1722, Adams was the son of a Boston brewer, John Adams. He also served in important city posts, such as selectman. Samuel was educated at Harvard. He took over the brewery after his father's death. But he had little interest in running a brewery and quickly lost the business. Samuel supported himself with his income from minor government jobs. This gave him time to indulge his real passion, politics.

According to historian John Ferling, Adams joined many political clubs that had sprung up across Boston. He could talk not only to well-to-do merchants but also to artisans and shopkeepers. He spoke at dinners and club meetings, and organized political events. Adams helped to motivate many of his listeners into protesters during the Stamp Act crisis.

Perhaps his most effective organizing tool was the Sons of Liberty, which he founded in Boston at this time. As Ferling has written, "It could be a medium for unleashing rampages in Boston's cobblestone streets, if necessary. But it was also a vehicle for preventing disorder and possible violence, for the Sons of Liberty was an organization that Adams . . . could carefully control and direct."[6] Patriots in other cities began to establish similar groups during the 1760s.

symbol of British rule. "Nothing remained but the bare walls and floors," Hutchinson later wrote.[7] Similar incidents occurred in other colonial cities. Demonstrators even tried to burn Benjamin Franklin's home in Philadelphia because he had supported the Stamp Act.

In October 1765, delegates from nine colonies met in New York at the Stamp Act Congress. The idea of a congress had been suggested by Massachusetts's delegates. The Congress reaffirmed the belief that Parliament did not have the right to tax the colonies without their consent and representation. While the congress was meeting, colonial merchants had also refused to import British goods. This boycott hurt merchants in Britain. They began pressuring Parliament to repeal the Stamp Act. British leaders also recognized that the colonists had also prevented any taxes from being collected. Stamp collectors had been frightened by mass protests. They had resigned their positions.

The Stamp Act was finally repealed in 1766, but Parliament reserved the right to pass other taxes.

The Townshend Duties

In England, many politicians were growing angrier with the attitudes of the colonists. The divisions between colonists and British politicians grew even greater when the Townshend Duties were passed in 1767. In London, Benjamin Franklin served as an agent and lobbyist for several of the colonies. He appeared before Parliament to talk about taxes. In his testimony, Franklin drew a distinction between internal taxes and duties on imports.

Franklin thought that duties on imports might be accepted in the colonies. But internal taxes like the Stamp Act, he said, would never be accepted. Charles Townshend, Chancellor of the Exchequer—Britain's head of the treasury—agreed with Franklin's viewpoint. He proposed to tax imports, such as paint, paper, glass, and tea. These were the so-called Townshend Duties.

Townshend may have seen a difference between internal taxes and import duties. However, most colonists did not agree. Once again, Massachusetts led the colonial protest against the new measure. Samuel Adams and James Otis composed the Massachusetts Circular Letter. They stated that Parliament did not have the right to impose the Townshend Duties.

In Pennsylvania, a member of the colonial assembly, John Dickinson, took a similar position. He issued a pamphlet called *Letters from a Farmer in Pennsylvania*. It was widely read throughout the American colonies. In the pamphlet, Dickinson denied "the power of parliament to lay upon these colonies any 'tax' whatever."[8] Once again, the colonists resorted to a boycott against English imports. Parliament eventually decided to repeal the new taxes. Each time Parliament passed a new tax, the colonists protested. And each time, Parliament backed down and repealed the tax. This action emboldened the colonists to take further action.

Meanwhile, in 1768, the ship *Liberty*, owned by wealthy Boston merchant John Hancock, was taken by British officials. They accused Hancock of smuggling Madeira into Boston. Protests broke out in Boston. Troops were moved into the city to deal with the protests. While the troops remained in the city, tensions rose between the British army and local citizens. On March 5, 1770, the situation finally boiled over. Around eight in the evening, a mob of three hundred Bostonians confronted a small force of English troops. Suddenly the soldiers began shooting. Five people were killed and many others were wounded. Anti-British colonists immediately began calling the incident the Boston Massacre. Samuel Adams demanded that British troops be removed from Boston. The troops were transported from the city to islands in the harbor. Those involved in the incident were tried in October 1770. Only two were convicted of manslaughter. Nevertheless, the Boston Massacre had increased colonial anger against the British.

The Conflict Grows

Attitudes on both sides of the Atlantic were hardening. Men like George Washington believed that their freedom was being undermined by the British parliament.[9] Others saw the Navigation Acts as an effort to ruin colonial tobacco planters by forcing them to sell only to Britain.[10] In 1773, Parliament gave Washington and other leaders a new reason to worry. The British government passed the Tea Act. Under this law, the British East India Company was given a monopoly on importing tea to the American colonies. The price of tea was set very low. Parliament believed this would appeal to colonial tea drinkers. However, it hurt colonial merchants. They had been smuggling tea from Holland and could no longer make any money on it.

Protests against the Tea Act broke out across the colonies. In New York, huge protests prevented a ship from leaving its cargo of tea on the wharves. In Boston, a group of two thousand protesters was organized by Samuel Adams and his associates. They lit up the darkened piers with their torches on the night of December 16, 1773. Meanwhile, about thirty men, dressed as Mohawk Indians, marched onto the tea ships in Boston harbor. They broke open the chests of tea. Then they hurled the broken chests into the

This musket was used by one of the colonies' many Committees of Safety. Committees of Safety were colonial groups that acted as temporary governments during the turbulent times before and during the Revolution.

The Rise of Alexander Hamilton

Alexander Hamilton was born on the Caribbean island of Nevis in 1755. Nevis was a British colony, covered in large sugar plantations. When he was about thirteen, Hamilton went to work for the import-export firm of Beekman and Cruger. Hamilton was very bright and learned the business quickly. As a result, he was put in charge of the Nevis office at the age of sixteen. The merchants who worked with Hamilton paid for the young man to travel to North America to attend college. Hamilton arrived in 1772.

While attending King's College (now Columbia University) in New York he worked at another merchant firm, Kortright and Company, a sugar importer. At Kortright, Hamilton was introduced to men who were members of the Sons of Liberty. Hamilton soon became involved in the turmoil over the Tea Act. In 1774, he may have participated in a demonstration that prevented any tea from being unloaded at New York harbor. At a huge gathering in 1774, Hamilton spoke out against the "enemies of America," and the "alarming state of [American] liberties."[11] He also published a pamphlet titled *A Full Vindication of the Measures of Congress*. The pamphlet supported the actions of the First Continental Congress. As war broke out in 1775, Hamilton joined the New York militia. He later raised an artillery company. At age twenty-one, he was appointed captain of artillery.

water, ruining the contents. The East India Company lost about one million dollars worth of tea.[12]

Parliament was furious. British political leaders struck back with a series of Coercive Acts. Americans called them the Intolerable Acts. Boston harbor was closed to all commerce. Food could not be imported by sea. In addition, the colonial assembly was ordered not to meet. The Boston Committee of Correspondence, established during the crises of the 1760s, contacted similar committees in other colonies. They organized support for the people of Boston in the other colonies. Some colonies sent food to the city's inhabitants. Many colonists were also extremely angry that Britain should violate the traditional rights of a colonial assembly to meet and pass laws. The Intolerable Acts helped unite many colonists in support of armed resistance against Britain.

In 1774, colonial delegates traveled to Philadelphia to hold the First Continental Congress. Among the delegates were George Washington and Samuel Adams. Beginning in September, fifty-six representatives met in Philadelphia's Carpenters' Hall. Once again, the colonies agreed to support a boycott of English imports. But this time, they went a step further. The delegates decided that the militia in every colony should be put "upon a proper footing."[13] Militia were groups of soldiers maintained by each colony for protection. Militiamen in Massachusetts were called "Minutemen," because they were expected to be ready

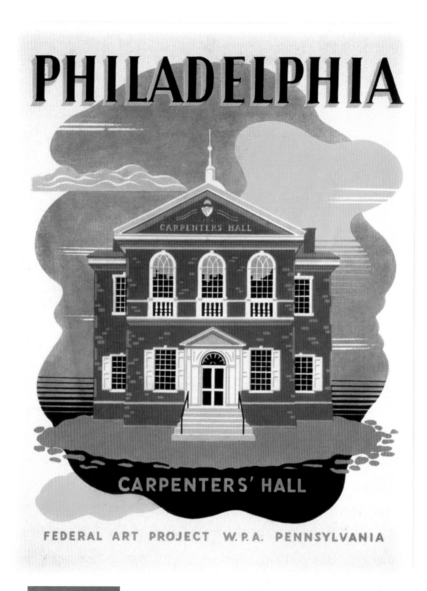

PHILADELPHIA

CARPENTERS' HALL

FEDERAL ART PROJECT W. P. A. PENNSYLVANIA

The First Continental Congress met in Carpenters' Hall in Philadelphia.

to defend their communities at a minute's notice. The colonies were clearly preparing to defend themselves.

The Coming of Independence

In England, the government, led by Lord North, also believed that war was likely. King George III was not willing to see Britain back down as the government had done during the 1760s. As the king remarked, "blows must decide whether they [the colonies] are to be subject to this country or independent."[14]

Meanwhile, in Boston, the British had appointed a military governor for Massachusetts, General Thomas Gage. He had decided to send troops to capture a store of ammunition in Concord and to arrest patriots John Hancock and Samuel Adams for treason. On April 19, 1775, British soldiers marched toward Concord. The night before, patriots William Dawes and Paul Revere had warned Hancock, Adams, and militia members throughout the countryside that the British were on their way. They intended to capture a store of colonial powder used in muskets. Along the way, the British Redcoats ran into a small group of farmers on the Lexington green. Firing broke out and eight militiamen were killed. The Redcoats continued their march into Concord. By the time they arrived a much larger force of militia had assembled. A small battle broke out at North Bridge. Three British soldiers were killed. The rest of the troops began to retreat to Boston.

But along the way, they were fired on by militiamen hiding behind bushes and stone walls. As many as sixty

A colonial soldier wore a three-cornered hat called a tricorn hat. The hat above dates back to the American Revolution.

British soldiers were killed before the rest of the British forces finally reached the safety of Boston. Outside the city, a militia from Massachusetts and the other New England colonies began to gather. Eventually this army reached sixteen thousand strong.

While fighting had broken out in Massachusetts, a Second Continental Congress had been called together in Philadelphia. The delegates decided to create a new Continental Army to carry on the resistance against England. This army included troops drawn from all the colonies. At the Congress, George Washington was

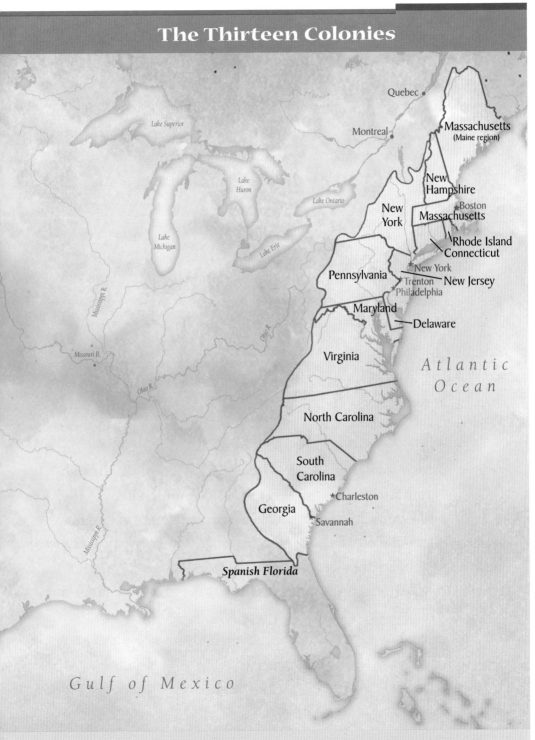

The Thirteen Colonies

Quebec

Montreal

Massachusetts
(Maine region)

New
Hampshire

New
York

Massachusetts

★Boston

Rhode Island
Connecticut

★New York

Pennsylvania

Trenton★ — New Jersey

★Philadelphia

Maryland

Delaware

Virginia

North Carolina

South
Carolina

★Charleston

Georgia

Savannah

Spanish Florida

Atlantic
Ocean

Gulf of Mexico

Lake Superior

Lake
Huron

Lake Ontario

Lake
Michigan

Lake Erie

Mississippi R.

Missouri R.

Ohio R.

Ohio R.

Mississippi R.

By 1775, the thirteen British colonies took up most of the eastern seaboard.

selected as commander-in-chief of the new army. Washington's experience in the French and Indian War impressed many of his colleagues. Delegates from New England, whose troops were already near Boston, supported a commander from Virginia. This gave the new army broad leadership. The choice of Washington also helped ensure support from the Southern colonies.

Before Washington could reach Boston, a battle had already occurred there. American troops were supposed to occupy Bunker Hill to bombard the British in Boston. Instead they occupied nearby Breed's Hill. On June 17, British troops attacked the American position at Breed's Hill. After successive charges, the British regulars finally managed to drive off the colonial army. Though the British took the hill, they lost almost twice as many men as the Americans. Although the engagement was fought on Breed's Hill, it came to be known as the Battle of Bunker Hill.

While General Washington took command in Boston, delegates at the Second Continental Congress submitted a petition to King George III. Written mainly by John Dickinson, the petition asked the king to make efforts to restore peace between Britain and its colonies. In November, the so-called Olive Branch Petition was rejected by King George III. The king regarded the Americans as rebels.

In January 1776, Thomas Paine issued a pamphlet called *Common Sense*. It immediately became a best seller throughout the colonies. Paine rejected the idea of monarchy, the concept of nobility, and the power of the

British parliament. He called on Americans to govern themselves and predicted that they could defeat the British in a long war. By spring and early summer 1776, many Americans recognized that a war for independence was inevitable. As a final step, Congress approved a Declaration of Independence on July 4, 1776.

In the face of a common threat, Americans had shown their ability to cooperate and work together. A similar situation had arisen during the French and Indian

Thomas Paine

Thomas Paine was born in England in 1737. He held minor government positions before meeting Benjamin Franklin in 1774. On Franklin's advice, Paine left England and sailed for America. In 1775, he published a pamphlet criticizing slavery in the colonies. He also became coeditor of the *Pennsylvania Magazine*.

His pamphlet, called *Common Sense*, was published in 1776 and was widely read throughout the American colonies. More than 500,000 copies were sold. Paine argued that independence was only a matter of time. The American colonies and Britain, he said, had grown out of touch with each other. His words had a strong influence on the political leaders who wrote the Declaration of Independence. After the war, Paine returned to England. Later he traveled to France, then back to America. He died in New York City in 1809.

This famous painting by John Trumbull shows the signing of the Declaration of Independence.

War. Americans decided to declare their independence, based on rights that had been exercised in the colonies for generations. That is, they believed in the right to decide many issues for themselves through their elected representatives. In the past, when these rights had been violated, American colonists refused to submit. When these same rights were threatened in 1775–1776, Americans once again refused to submit and rose up to declare their independence.

A New Nation

The American Revolution began in New England, but the conflict quickly spread to the other colonies in 1776. Over the next two years, decisive battles were fought in New York, New Jersey, and Pennsylvania. By the late 1770s, warfare had overrun the Southern colonies. In 1781, the British were defeated at Yorktown, Virginia, bringing an end to the major campaigns of the war. Once independence had been secured, American political leaders began to reshape the government and create a new constitution.

War in the North

While the Second Continental Congress was meeting in Philadelphia, the British launched an attack on New York City. British ships carrying an army of thirty-two thousand arrived off New York in July. Facing them, General Washington had gathered an army of about twenty-eight thousand troops. General William Howe, commanding the British, established his camp on Staten Island outside New York City. Both commanders recognized the importance of New York. It was a leading colonial port, critical to the American war effort.

Washington split his forces between New York City and nearby Long Island. Late in August, he fortified his position on Long Island to beat back a British attack. However, Washington's main army was out-flanked and almost surrounded during the Battle of Long Island, on August 27, 1776. American militia-man Joseph Plumb Martin remembered seeing some of his retreating comrades being shelled by British artillery. They tried to escape across a pond but were pelted with a "shower of hail," Martin said. "When they came out of the water and mud to us, looking like water rats, it was a truly pitiful sight. Many of them were killed in the pond, and more were drowned."[1]

Washington's army retreated to the north. They were struck by the British outside of New York. By this time, many of the militiamen had little taste left for fighting. "Amongst other things," wrote militiaman Garret Watts, "I confess I was amongst the first that fled. The cause of that I cannot tell, except that every-one I saw was about to do the same.... Officers and men joined in the flight. I threw away my gun. ...."[2] Washington abandoned New York, leaving the city to General Howe.

During the fall of 1776, General Howe chased Washington's army out of New York, through New Jersey. Washington retreated across the Delaware River into Pennsylvania. In this dark hour of the war, Thomas Paine published his pamphlet *The Crisis*. "These are the times that try men's souls," Paine wrote. "The summer soldier and the sunshine patriot will, in this crisis, shrink from the service of his country; but he that stands it now, deserves the love and thanks of man and woman."[3] By this time, many of the American militia had gone home. Washington's army had been reduced to only five thousand men. Paine's words, however, convinced many of them to continue fighting.

During the French and Indian War, George Washington had learned how to keep an army together in the face of terrible odds. On December 25, 1776, his army recrossed the Delaware River during a cold,

This chest was used by George Washington when his army made camp. In it, he had plates, silverware, and other items he needed.

It was a cold night when Washington and his men crossed the icy waters of the Delaware River into New Jersey. In real life, he probably would not have been standing in the boat as it crossed the river's rough waters.

snowy Christmas night. The following morning the Continental Army struck a small contingent of Hessians, the German mercenaries hired by the British, stationed at Trenton, New Jersey. The Hessians had been celebrating late the previous evening. In the morning, they were totally surprised and quickly routed. On January 3, 1777, Washington advanced north to Princeton, New Jersey. There his army won another victory. The Continental Army, which seemed completely lost, had suddenly shown that they could defeat the enemy. The British quickly retreated to northern New Jersey.

Victory and Defeat

In 1777, the British planned to follow up their capture of New York with an even more daring plan. A British army, numbering about seven thousand men, left Canada in June. There was a direct route by water down Lake Champlain to Lake George and the Hudson River to Albany. Led by General John Burgoyne, the British hoped to capture Albany and split off New York from the New England colonies.

By July, the British had taken control of Lake Champlain and Lake George. But after initial success, the campaign slowly encountered trouble. American militia under the command of French and Indian War veteran John Stark defeated a British force at Bennington, Vermont, in August. In the Mohawk River Valley to the west, another British army was beaten at almost the same time.

By September, General Burgoyne had staked out a position on the Hudson River north of Albany. However, his army had been reduced in numbers. Meanwhile, he faced a larger American army under the command of another French and Indian War veteran, General Horatio Gates. General Gates had served alongside Daniel Morgan in that war. In 1777, Morgan joined Gates with a contingent of crack riflemen to face Burgoyne. At two battles fought near Saratoga during September and October 1777, Burgoyne was soundly defeated. Morgan's men played a key role in American victory. On October 16, 1777, Burgoyne was forced to surrender his army.

General Burgoyne's surrender at Saratoga was a turning point in the American Revolution.

The result was electrifying. Benjamin Franklin had been sent to Paris to persuade the French government to assist the American cause. He had successfully charmed the French government ministers and the aristocrats. They were fascinated with Franklin. As his biographer Gordon Wood wrote, "In French eyes Franklin came to symbolize America as no single person in history ever has."[4] The French were also eager to avenge their losses in the French and Indian War. However, they were not certain that the American army could defeat the British. Saratoga changed everything. Late in 1777, France recognized American independence. The French began to send ships and soldiers to the United States in support of the Continental Army.

The War Shifts South

While the American army defeated the British at Saratoga, British General Howe had taken a large force south to attack Philadelphia. Howe successfully outmaneuvered General Washington's forces at the Battle of Brandywine. The British entered the American capital in September 1777. General Howe may have thought the American government would surrender with the loss of its capital. This usually occurred in European warfare. But the Continental Congress simply moved to a new location in Pennsylvania. In 1778, Howe evacuated Philadelphia and returned to New York.

Meanwhile, the American Revolution shifted to

The Battle of King's Mountain

At King's Mountain, South Carolina, in October 1780, patriot militia attacked British loyalists. An army of eleven hundred Loyalists—also called Tories—were under the command of Major Patrick Ferguson. James Collins, an American militia-man, recalled that they charged up the hill against the Tory position. "The shot of the enemy soon began to pass over us like hail; the first shock was quickly over, and for my own part, I was soon in profuse sweat. My lot happened to be in the center, where the severest part of the battle was fought."

The militia had to charge the enemy three times. "We took to the hill a third time; the enemy gave way" Collins recalled. "They soon threw down their arms and surrendered. . . . the dead lay in heaps on all sides, while the groans of the wounded were heard in every direction. I could not help turning away from the scene before me, with horror, and though exulting in victory, could not refrain from shedding tears."[5] Ferguson's entire force was either captured or killed.

the South. A large group of loyalists—Americans who remained loyal to Great Britain—lived in the Southern colonies. The British hoped to stir them to rebellion by a successful invasion of Georgia and the Carolinas. The strategy almost worked. Savannah, Georgia, was captured by the British in 1778. Then the British captured Charles Town, South Carolina, in 1780. After these victories, the British gradually took control of much of the South. However, American patriots continued to fight back.

The tide of battle gradually turned against the British in the South. During 1781, American troops led by General Nathaniel Greene drove the British out of the Carolinas. A British commander, General

Charles Cornwallis, led his army to Virginia. At Yorktown, along the Virginia coast, Cornwallis hoped to be protected by the British navy. Instead, he was trapped. Cornwallis was surrounded by a combined force of American and French troops on land and the French navy near the coast. In October 1781, Cornwallis surrendered. This ended the major campaigns of the American Revolution.

In 1783, America and Great Britain signed the Treaty of Paris officially ending the war. The British formally recognized the independence of the United States of America. Among the American peace commissioners were John Adams and Benjamin Franklin.

The surrender of the British to the Americans astounded much of Europe.

A New Constitution

The United States had achieved its independence. But the central government was weak. During the Revolution, the Second Continental Congress had guided the thirteen American states. The Congress wrote a framework of government, known as the articles of Confederation. Under the Articles, the United States Congress was the main organ of the central government. However, most of the power remained with the states. Each state decided whether to pay any taxes to support the Congress. Under the Articles, Congress also lacked the power to deal with foreign nations.

After the war, Britain prevented American merchants from trading with the British colonies in the Caribbean. Spain had a large empire in the Southwest. The Spanish closed the Mississippi River to American commerce. The port of New Orleans, a Spanish colony, was shut to American farmers in the west. They could not ship their produce down the Mississippi River to Europe. In addition, England maintained troops and manned forts on the Great Lakes. These outposts prevented more American settlers from moving westward. Congress was too weak to deal with any of these problems.

Some American political leaders realized that the time had come to act. Among them was James Madison, a young Congressman from Virginia. He was joined by Alexander Hamilton, who had become a successful political figure in New York. George

Washington also realized that the future of the United States was in jeopardy.

In 1786, a farmers' revolt broke out in Massachusetts. The revolt was led by a Revolutionary War veteran named Daniel Shays. The revolt occurred because many farmers were in debt and they were about to lose their farms. Shays and his followers tried to prevent the local courts from taking away their farms. Shays' Rebellion was stopped by local government troops. However, Washington feared that similar revolts might spread to other states. Congress, under the Articles of Confederation, lacked an army to stamp out a revolution.

In 1787, a group of fifty-five delegates from the American states met in Philadelphia. Their mission was to improve the Articles of Confederation. However, the delegates soon realized that the existing framework could not create the type of central or

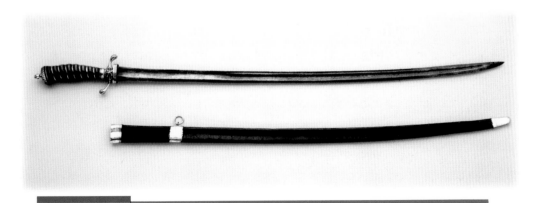

General George Washington wore this sword at his side during the American Revolution.

federal government that was needed. Therefore, they began working on an entirely new framework of government. The Constitution called for a much stronger central government—including a President, Congress, and Supreme Court. The Congress would consist of two houses, the House and the Senate, which would share lawmaking power. This was much like the two houses in the British parliament and the Iroquois Confederacy.

Under the new federal system, the states retained some of their independence. However, they were required to subordinate much of their power to the central government.

The signing and ratification of the Constitution established the government of the United States that we know today.

The Constitution of the United States

The new Constitution was approved by the delegates in Philadelphia and later ratified by the states. It created a balanced government, similar to the framework that existed during the colonial period. A Bill of Rights was added to the original Constitution to safeguard many of the liberties that had become so important during the colonial period. These rights included freedom of speech, freedom to worship, and a law preventing the quartering of soldiers in private homes.

In many ways the new Constitution was the culmination of those struggles that had formed such an integral part of the American colonial era.

1585 First Roanoke colony established in present-day North Carolina.

1607 Jamestown established in Virginia.

1616 John Rolfe grows tobacco in Virginia.

1619 Virginia House of Burgesses holds first meeting; Africans first brought to Virginia.

1620 Pilgrims land in Plymouth, Massachusetts.

1630 Massachusetts Bay colony established.

1631 Maryland established by Lord Baltimore.

1637 Pequot War breaks out in New England.

1664 The English conquer the Dutch New Netherland.

1675 King Philip's War breaks out in New England.

1682 William Penn creates settlement at Philadelphia.

1712 Slave revolt breaks out in New York City.

1733 Colony of Georgia founded.

1739 Slave revolt occurs at Stono River, South Carolina.

1744 King George's War begins.

1754 French and Indian War breaks out in Ohio Valley.

1759 British troops capture French capital at Quebec.

1764 Sugar Act passed by Parliament.

1765 Stamp Act imposed on American colonies.

1767 Townshend Duties passed by Parliament.

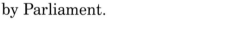

1770 Boston Massacre occurs.

1773 Tea Act, passed by Parliament, is followed by Boston Tea Party.

1774 Parliament closes Boston port; First Continental Congress meets.

1775 Second Continental Congress meets; American Revolution breaks out in Massachusetts.

1776 Declaration of Independence signed.

1777 American forces win battle at Saratoga; France recognizes American independence.

1781 American and French forces win Battle of Yorktown.

1783 Treaty of Paris signed between Great Britain and United States.

1787 Constitutional Convention meets in Philadelphia.

Chapter One   A Declaration

1. John Ferling, *A Leap in the Dark: The Struggle to Create the American Republic* (New York: Oxford University Press, 2003), p. 163.

2. Ibid., p. 169.

3. A. J. Langguth, *Patriots: The Men Who Started the American Revolution* (New York: Simon and Schuster, 1988), p. 363.

4. Ferling, p. 167.

Chapter Two   Opening a New Land

1. Daniel Richter, *Facing East from Indian Country: A Native History of Early America* (Cambridge, Mass.: Harvard University Press, 2001), p. 7.

2. Ibid., p. 63.

3. Ibid., p. 52.

4. Lee Sultzman, "Iroquois History," n.d., <http://www.tolatsga.org/iro.html> (July 7, 2005).

5. John C. Mohawk, "Iroquois Confederacy," *Encyclopedia of North American Indians*, n.d., <http://college.hmco.com/history/readerscomp/naind/html/na_017500_iroquoisconf.htm> (July 7, 2005).

6. Ibid.

Chapter Three   The New English Settlements

1. Alan Taylor, *American Colonies* (New York: Viking, 2001), p. 130.

2. Ibid., p. 131.

3. Ibid., p. 134.

4. Richard Middleton, *Colonial America: A History, 1585–1776*, Second Edition (Malden, Mass.: Blackwell Publishers, 1996), p. 61.

5. Taylor, p. 139.

6. Middleton, p. 80.

7. Taylor, p. 161.

8. Ibid., p. 172.

9. Daniel Richter, *Facing East from Indian Country: A Native History of Early America* (Cambridge, Mass.: Harvard University Press, 2001), p. 59.

10. "Biography," *Anne Hutchinson*, December 5, 2002, <http://www.annehutchinson.com/anne_hutchinson_biography_003.htm> (July 7, 2005).

11. Ibid., pp. 45–46.

12. Taylor, p. 203.

13. Daniel J. Boorstin, *The Americans, The Colonial Experience* (New York: Random House, 1958), p. 43.

14. Middleton, p. 165.

Chapter Four   Trade, Agriculture, and Slavery

1. Carl Bridenbaugh, *Cities in the Wilderness* (New York: Knopf, 1968), p. 303.

2. Richard Middleton, *Colonial America: A History, 1585–1776*, Second Edition (Malden, Mass.: Blackwell Publishers, 1996), p. 226.

3. Cathy Matson, *Merchants and Empire: Trading in Colonial New York* (Baltimore: Johns Hopkins University Press, 1998), p. 227.

4. Ibid.

5. Alan Taylor, *American Colonies* (New York: Viking, 2001), p. 311.

6. Bridenbaugh, p. 331.

7. Matson, pp. 150–151.

8. Gordon S. Wood, "The Shopper's Revolution," *New York Review of Books*, June 10, 2004, p. 26.

9. Bridenbaugh, p. 345.

10. "Peter Kalm on Albany," *The Colonial Albany Social Project*, February 6, 2003, <http://www.nysm.nysed.gov/albany/art/kalm.html> (July 7, 2005).

11. Matson, p. 223.

12. Bridenbaugh, p. 180.

13. Ibid., pp. 143, 303.

14. Jay Coughtry, "The Notorious Triangle," n.d. <http://www.cyberspace.org/~jh/wgh/coughtry.html> (October 27, 2005).

15. "Alexander Falconbridge's account of the slave trade," *Africans in America*, n.d., <http://www.pbs.org/wgbh/aia/part1/1h281.html> (July 7, 2005).

16. Herbert S. Klein, The *Atlantic Slave Trade* (Cambridge, England: Cambridge University Press, 1999), p. 150.

17. Ira Berlin, *Many Thousands Gone: The First Two Centuries of Slavery in North America* (Cambridge, Mass.: Harvard University Press, 1998), p. 369.

18. Ibid., p. 110.

19. Ibid., pp. 369–370.

20. Middleton, p. 217.

21. Taylor, p. 237.

22. Berlin, p. 117.

Chapter Five   Colonial Society

1. Carl Bridenbaugh, *Cities in the Wilderness* (New York: Knopf, 1968), pp. 347, 441.

2. Ira Berlin, *Many Thousands Gone: The First Two Centuries of Slavery in North America* (Cambridge, Mass.: Harvard University Press, 1998), p. 115.

3. "William Byrd's Diary," *Africans in America*, n.d., <http://www.pbs.org/wgbh/aia/part1/1h283t. html> (July 7, 2005).

4. Bridenbaugh, pp. 379–380.

5. Richard Middleton, *Colonial America: A History, 1585–1776*, Second Edition (Malden, Mass.: Blackwell Publishers, 1996), p. 245.

6. "Interesting Facts," *Benjamin Franklin: An Enlightened American*, n.d., <http://library.think quest.org/22254/frintfac.htm> (July 7, 2005).

7. Daniel J. Boorstin, *The Americans, The Colonial Experience* (New York: Random House, 1958), p. 308.

8. Alan Taylor, *American Colonies* (New York: Viking, 2001), pp. 316–317.

9. Ibid., p. 321.

10. Middleton, p. 263.

11. LoveToKnow, Inc., "History of Colonial Georgia," *Our Country*, © 2002–2003, <http://www.public-bookshelf.com/public_html/Our_Country_Vol_1/ historyco_fj.html> (July 7, 2005).

Chapter Six   Colonial Government

1. Daniel J. Boorstin, *The Americans, The Colonial Experience* (New York: Random House, 1958), p. 128.

2. Ibid., p. 109.

3. Carl Bridenbaugh, *Cities in the Wilderness* (New York: Knopf, 1968), p. 156.

4. Richard Middleton, *Colonial America: A History, 1585–1776*, Second Edition (Malden, Mass.: Blackwell Publishers, 1996), p. 372.

5. Fred Anderson, *Crucible of War* (New York: Knopf, 2000), p. 29.

6. Ibid., p. 44.

7. Ibid., pp. 100–102.

Chapter Seven   The Coming of Independence

1. John Ferling, *A Leap in the Dark: The Struggle to Create the American Republic* (New York: Oxford University Press, 2003), p. 28.

2. Fred Anderson, *Crucible of War* (New York: Knopf, 2000), pp. 469–470.

3. Ibid., pp. 589–594.

4. Gordon S. Wood, *The Americanization of Benjamin Franklin* (New York: Penguin Press, 2004), p. 107.

5. "Patrick Henry's Resolutions," *The Library of Virginia*, December 20, 2005, <http://www.lva.lib.va.us/whatwedo/k12/psd/colony/henry1765.htm> (January 2006).

6. Ferling, p. 66.

7. Ibid., p. 39.

8. Ibid., p. 70.

9. Ibid., p. 82.

10. Ibid., p. 84.

11. Willard Sterne Randall, *Alexander Hamilton* (New York: HarperCollins, 2003), p. 78.

12. Ferling, p. 106.

13. Ibid, p. 121.

14. Ibid., pp. 123–124.

Chapter Eight   A New Nation

1. Ray Raphael, *A People's History of the American Revolution* (New York: The New Press, 2001), p. 68.

2. Ibid., p. 69.

3. A. J. Langguth, *Patriots: The Men Who Started The American Revolution* (New York: Simon and Schuster, 1988), p. 401.

4. Gordon S. Wood, *The Americanization of Benjamin Franklin* (New York: Penguin Press, 2004), p. 180.

5. Raphael, p. 80.

almshouse—Place where the poor lived and worked.

apprentice—A young boy who learned a trade from an artisan.

barracoon—Slave pen used to prevent slaves from escaping while they waited on the African coast.

indentured servants—Colonists in North America who worked for a master for a period of years in return for having their passage paid.

Middle Passage—Voyage from Africa across the Atlantic by slave ships.

overseer—White supervisor of slaves on a large plantation.

slave codes—Laws in Southern colonies to restrict lives of slaves.

slave driver—Black supervisor of slave gangs on a plantation.

swaddling clothes—Strips of linen wrapped around a baby, meant to support the back.

tenant farmer—A farmer who rented property from a landlord.

Tories—Americans who remained loyal to England during the Revolutionary War.

vestry—Unit of local government in the Southern colonies.

Axelrod-Contrada, Joan. *A Historical Atlas of Colonial America*. New York: Rosen Publishing Group, 2005.

Bial, Raymond. *Early American Villages*. New York: Children's Press, 2004.

Bjornlund, Lydia. *Women of Colonial America*. San Diego: Lucent Books, 2004.

Keller, Kristin Thoennes. *The Slave Trade in Early America*. Mankato, Minn.: Capstone Press, 2004.

Nelson, Sheila. *The Northern Colonies: The Quest for Freedom, 1600–1700*. Philadelphia: Mason Crest Publishers, 2005.

———. *The Original United States of America: Americans Discover the Meaning of Independence 1770–1800*. Philadelphia: Mason Crest Publishers, 2005.

———. *The Southern Colonies: The Quest for Prosperity*. Mason Crest Publishers, 2004.

Ryan, Michael C., ed. *Living in Colonial America*. Farmington Hills, Mich.: Greenhaven Press, 2004.

Schanzer, Rosalyn. *George vs. George: The Revolutionary War as Seen from Both Sides*. National Geographic Children's Books, 2004.

Stanley, George E. *The European Settlement of North America (1492–1754)*. Milwaukee, Wis.: World Almanac Library, 2005.

Wilcox, Charlotte. *Games and Leisure in Colonial America*. Mankato, Minn.: Blue Earth Books, 2004.

Wilds, Mary C. *A Colonial Craftsman*. Detroit: Thomson/Gale, 2005.

Africans in America, Part 1
  <http://www.pbs.org/wgbh/aia/part1/
  narrative.html>

**America's Story from America's Library:
  Colonial America (1492–1763)**
  <http://www.americaslibrary.gov/cgi-bin/page.
  cgi/jb/colonial>

Colonial Williamsburg
  <http://www.history.org>